Lies always *RISE* when someone dies…

By:
HONESTGYRL LEMON

Copyright © 2020 M. Battles-Lemon
All rights reserved.
ISBN: **9780578849324**

DEDICATION

This book is dedicated to #myoneandonly. I knew when I brought you into this world, I wanted you to have a great life. Thank you for making me a better person. I am so blessed to have been chosen to be your mother. 'If the sky is your limit My, that means there are no limits -Mom

To my husband, Mr. JR Lemon III, thank you for pushing me to 'just do it and say 'eff' everybody else. You are what I needed, even when you snore! You are my **best** friend, love and family…we're in this thing called parenting and life together. LET'S GET IT
#migsandnem

ACKNOWLEDGMENTS

For all the people that I have met throughout my journey, thank you! **Everything** I have been through, accomplished, lost and regained were all stepping-stones used for my betterment. I learned from the places I have been and the people I met; from those who love me, and even those that tried hard to sabotage and break me, God is intentional! I already thanked Him for all of it. So, to you I want to say thank you because you gave me the opportunity of knowing the depth of my own strength.

-Migs

Prologue: Jhonnie

'I'm too emotional they say...'

I'm learning in my adult life; my family is just as dysfunctional as any other family. Blood, water, like and love related alike...all of them, everybody! Dysfunctional in one way or another

My life, I quickly learned was the results of my elders and their full life of lies and bad choices. I somehow managed to still make it through semi-alright, for the most part.

Long story short, like with any other family; it all started to come out after my grandmom's funeral. The first slip was how my twin cousins aren't technically my blood cousins; but that changed nothing. We were too tight.

"Secrets and lies always rise when someone dies" she said.

She being Sofiya Bradshaw, my childhood friend's Godmom, who at one point was my uncle's lady-friend and now, well I'm still adjusting to our newest connection.

Sofiya told me her story and her years with Joshua. Now, I had heard over the years, *the story of Joshua* but I heard it a little different from the lady formerly known as my mother. According to her, *she* was the *love of Joshua's life,* so what if he was Sofiya's husband. Who cared? Damn sure, not her...

Thankfully for Sofiya, when shit got *really* bad, someone called in a tip to the authorities. The next thing you know, Joshua's facing federal time.

He tried to continue business as usual without Sofiya but soon after his sentencing, Joshua's health started to decline. For whatever reason, he felt the need to come clean to Sofiya about his dirt and then made her his Power of Attorney. Joshua knew Sofiya was a good person, and she was a much better person than I would have been to him, if it were up to me.

Imagine my surprise when Sofiya told me the whole story of how when her husband died, she got almost everything, which I knew to be a lot of money and as well as property, jewelry and other stuff.

A few months after her come-up aka Joshua's demise behind the wall, word hit the street that my father was not my biological parent. How that whole scenario played out was crazy, it's a whole 'notha story...

But back to the mess that was her husband Joshua. Not only did he do her bad financially, but Joshua also ended up fathering twins with my Uncle Junie's estranged wife. He had been playing father to the children for years with Ant Nay, remember those twin cousins that ended up not being my blood cousins? Yeah, this was them.

So, let me help you out...My mother's brother, my Uncle Junie raised children that ended up being fathered by Sofiya's husband, Joshua aka Bully.

Plus, Joshua possibly had a baby with Celeste, which they believed to be me. Not only was Joshua with Ant Nay *and the woman formerly known as my mother,* but he was also doing his business through some lady named Estelle.

Now, after all of that, Joshua had the nerve to ask Sofiya to set up money for the children right after he got diagnosed with MS.

Sofiya was honest, "At first I didn't want too but if they were his children, then the money was rightfully theirs; no matter how they were conceived" she said.

Joshua wanted to leave two million dollars to be split equally and he wanted to purchase each of them a home. Now Joshua had the money, actual cash. This money authorities didn't find in their seizures. Joshua had money hidden in houses, but he didn't trust anyone to do the right thing with his stuff. Especially, after his one brother and mother stole paperwork to a few of our properties. He wanted to be extra careful with whatever remained.

As a part of the deal, in exchange for her release of the legit money. Joshua left his keys for Sofiya that went to different houses and properties. Sofiya described how each house had a safe of some sort with money in it. Joshua asked for Sofiya to adjust her life insurance beneficiaries to include Joshua's children, you know to keep it all looking legit. And that's what Sofiya did, she adjusted her life insurance beneficiaries to include Joshua's children.

She only left herself enough to appear to live comfortably.

The truth is, Sofiya is the first one that comes to mind when I think of people that are wealthy. I have seen her walk onto a car lot, pick a car and write a check. I've seen her buy a house on a walk through, she had *money*. And to think she was looked at as the stupid vengeful widow of a big-time drug dealer that only messed with her dead husband's kid mother's ex-husband out of spite. Yeah, after the dust settled, my Uncle Junie approached Sofiya, and she accepted his requests.

Can you imagine the disgust I felt for her husband? I remembered crying quietly as she sobbed while she told me her story. I pushed through but I could not stop the tears. I looked at my phone. It was three in the morning; we had been outside talking since ten o'clock at night.

Sofiya had made this man, he looked legit on paper, she helped him maintain a great life. Joshua appeared to be a successful businessman when he was nothing more than a dedicated street guy and that was how he treated her?

Sofiya and Joshua were always together so it was assumed they were married long before they actually tied the knot. She had spent years trying to get away from Bully. She wanted to get a divorce from him, but she knew he would never sign papers. So, she created a plan, she was trying to secure her and her unborn child's life. Right before the incident that caused Sofiya to go on the run, she put some things in place.

Sofiya shared how one time, Joshua had gotten arrested while driving through a strict township and they locked him up on some municipal warrants. While Joshua was in the *bing*, he needed Sofiya to get some documents to his attorney and she slipped another life insurance policy signature page into some papers that his attorney needed him to sign. Somehow the attorney caught wind of the paperwork. But by *that* time, the account was created, and payments were already being made on the policy. Joshua let her keep it but told her that even when he dies, the attorney would appeal the whole transaction and keep delaying it, so she would never get it. That put a damper on her 'safety net' plan.

Whew Chile I know it's a lot!

And I had to quickly learn there's sooooo much more to this story. One thing about Sofiya, she is smart. She knew enough to know to get a four-million-dollar life insurance policy on Joshua very early in their relationship. The policy that he claimed drove him to cheat with Ant Nay, the woman formerly known as my mother and Estelle, was the same policy he came back years later asking to use after making Sofiya his Power of Attorney, or POA, over for his children and other family's belongings.

"We fought bad behind that first policy" Sofiya put her glass down. "He vowed to never give me another dime" she wiped her eyes.

To that point, Sofiya was a kept woman, she did not work. She argued that she would be carrying their children in the future, the first signs of his legacy but it didn't work. Probably because he knew he had other children already, she just didn't know.

Sofiya was stressed just telling the story. I could see her energy shifting as she explained the situation. I listened as she repeated her plan to "hold everything down" financially if something happened to Joshua. Of course, he wasn't trying to hear it. He turned cold and calloused towards her.

I thought my story was crazy, here I was finding out my entire life was a lie but hearing her story and learning things about both of my families was crazy.

I'm glad I decided to move. I need something different; these past five years has been bananas. So, I'm just trying to enjoy my time with her. I had come to love our moments, I especially loved to hear about her life with Joshua, he was a real live wire. Their stories were the funniest on one hand but yet the saddest on the other.

"I'm hungry" she announced over the jazz that was playing on her stereo. "Let's go to the diner" she suggested as she grabbed her keys.

Sofiya was telling me why she ended things with Joshua. She described it as being her *final straw.*

Sofiya shared how he slept around but forbid her to even *live* anywhere else. So, she played his game until the night she *had* to go on the run.

"Don't let me forget, I have to tell you 'bout the night I thought I killed his dumb ass" she said with a straight face. "But we got all weekend for that...so now that I got you here and it's just us…"

She looked around, "Tell me how the hell you ended up with a damn *Murphy?"*

"Well, at that time, I had just beat my case. I had a couple *dollars* left, so I was out! I decided to take a trip" I looked at her as we pulled into the diner.

Sofiya chuckled, "I know that's right."

"Annnddd, I met him on the plane ride home. I initially only gave him the time of day because not only did he work hard to get the seat next to me, he smelled so good like I *knew* he smoked but he carried it well" I smiled remembering that moment.

"At first, I *haatteedd Logan, you know when I thought he ghosted me"* I looked over at her.

"Riiigght, right but now?" Sofiya asked.

"Are you kidding, he's my *favorite*" I laughed falling back into the booth.

Sofiya scoffed, "Uhn huh, only if my honeybun ain't around."

I laughed, "But they know that!! Everybody knows Levi is my favorite of the favorites" I smiled.

"So, tell me 'bout this here, *Bop"* she picked up her menu.

"Well which story do you want? Do you wanna hear about Bop, what happened between me and Fiki or how I *ended up with* a damn Murphy" I chuckled. "Because those are all very separate, although connecting at times, still very different stories. So, which one do you want?" I asked with a smirk.

"You ain't cute" she said dropping the menu.

She put the menu down, "Ok, just start from 'you beat your case, you go have *big fun'* out West, you come back, you meet a Murphy on the plane ride home...then what?" she unwrapped her straw and put it in her water.

"Then things were going good or so I thought, then outta nowhere, he ghosted me, so I took another trip...

Chapter 2: Jhonnie

It's like, 'I just can't seem to recover...'

Every time I get over one blow, here comes another head banger. And then people wonder why I tear shit up! I got a lot to be mad about! Let me take you back to about four-five-ish years ago.

I was just getting back from my family's house, when work started showing its ass so, I took another leave and spent nearly a month away from everybody. Almost doing time in the FEDS, then finding out your life was a total lie, can make you need some time alone to reflect and regroup.

Now that whole FEDS thing, I just knew I was going down. Then at the last hour, my ex changed his story, and I was able to walk away with some thangs. So yeah, I needed some space.

The time away was cool. I reconnected with a couple old friends, which means I was doing a lot of traveling and bouncing between places. Well during one of the times while on my way home, I met a guy named Logan Murphy.

He was a different type of dude than I was used too, he was younger than me. Not by much though, we're a year and some months apart. Now, I usually date older, but I was kinda feeling him. Then just when I was ready to be all about him, he ghosted me.

I had just accepted being *ghosted* when my Uncle Sammy called me back to town, and I was too ready to go.

My Uncle Sammy was the longtime boyfriend to my mom's sister, Judy. They had dated my entire life, then finally got married. I have pictures as a youngster with Uncle Sammy, so imagine my surprise at them finally getting married, when I was sixteen. Like, *Y'all wasn't already legit?*

I had two uncles from my mother's side: Uncle Junie and Uncle Sammy and I loved my OGs. My aunts were cool but my uncles?!?! They were my guys.

"Uncle Sammy, I was just down there" I reminded him.

He ignored my objections and continued with his directive. He said he needed and wanted to handle some business. He needed to make some changes to his will. According to Uncle Sammy, since he did not have any children, he wanted to leave everything to his favorite niece. One of his houses, some money and his stake in a business investment. The crazy part is when he first mentioned making me his benefactor after my dad died, I thought to myself, 'my uncle has a son' why would he leave anything to me.

I asked about his son, and he simply said, "MaJhonnie what did Uncle Sammy ask you to do?"

I quickly replied, "Yes sir" and told him I would be ready and waiting for his call. So, when he called me back to town a few months after I had recently returned from my post FEDS hiatus at his spot, I knew it must be time to hear another whammy.

Since my Dad passed, so much stuff has come out about my family. As much as I didn't want to leave with this chaos unraveling, I packed my bag, I checked in points to book my flight and I was off to see my Uncle Sammy and Ant Judy.

I called my best friend Rebecca; we had been friends since we were kids. I needed her to do me a favor, she owed me.

"Begs, I need a favor! Can you take care of Brutus and let the repair people in for me? I have to go see Uncle Sammy" I said into the receiver as I opened my drawer.

Again, oh my god is he okay" she asked.

I was rolling up clothes and putting them in my suitcase. "Yes, he's fine! Please remember to run a hot water bleach cycle *after* you're done with your clothes" I said moving around.

I ignored Rebecca's fake offense because she knows why I felt the need to say that.

"Oh my god Jhonnie that was one time" she objected to detailed instructions.

I went back to my rules, "Please stay on the second floor do not entertain on my floor" I paused to wait for her response.

"Really Jhonnie, ok but in my defense" she started to rehash it.

I cut her off, "Begs we don't even have too please just stay on the second floor" I concluded by asking Rebecca to repeat codes and systems.

I told her that my Ant Peachy was dropping Brutus off after his appointment at the groomers Friday.

"I hate that you really make us schedule pickups and drop offs for this damn dog like he's a real kid" she spat into the phone.

I hung up on her before she made me mad because she knows how much I love my dog. I would take him, but he bit Uncle Sammy's friends, so he's no longer welcomed.

I considered letting my mother know I was going but changed my mind when Uncle Sammy said that would possibly mean having to share stuff with my mom.

"Jhonnie, if you tell your mom you're coming, she's going to want to come and I love my sister-in-law, but I don't want her in my business" he said.

So, I figured I'll call her after we're done or when I get back.

I ordered my Uber and pulled my bag down the stairs. I said my goodbyes to Brutus and walked outside. I scrolled through my phone and pressed *New Thang* "heading to airport to see my Uncle."

A few minutes passed, "Hit me when you land" I smiled and put the phone in my bag. I was beginning to like him more than I expected. I scrolled down to *'Never Again'*, my ex. I wish he just woulda done right, the first or second time around.

OH SHIT!!

I hurried up and backed out of his messages as he typed 'hi'.

My phone chimed again, "Can I come see you" I rolled my eyes at my ex's request. I backed out of the screen and put my phone on airplane mode.

The flight was cool, I was happy to be back. I got in late after a delay, so I went right to sleep. I was having lunch at my uncle's house the next day when my phone rang, "Oh excuse me Unc I need to take this" I said backing up from the table.

I stepped outside, "I am so sorry I really just got myself together, but I'm out of town" I explained.

Corey, my ex-fiancé cleared his throat, "It's cool MaJhonnie" he replied. Corey had been calling me lately wanting to talk. I was *not* excited to *hear him out*.

I hadn't talked to Corey since I walked out of the airport. No wait, I did call when I heard he was marrying his last *baby mom*. The one he kept lying about even dealing with, so he naturally denied paternity but changed his tune when those papers came...

He really tried to keep me in limbo, I couldn't wait anymore so I moved on. Initially, I told him we were on hold until them results came back, but the more I sat with it I asked myself, *'What am I waiting for?*

This jerk cheated on me with not one but two women and might have both these broads pregnant? Naw I'm out!

Of course, I came to that revelation walking off the cruise ship from a twelve-day European cruise.

He covered the cost of the best vacation experience ever.

Corey took me on a "Let me make it up to you" sixteen-day vacation with him.

Pulling down my sunglasses looking at all those that asked, "How could I possibly go anywhere with him after he did what he did?"

Please, don't judge me! Everybody has their way to heal and mine is through trips, money and expensive gifts.

Of course, we had separate rooms. I'm no fool, we were definitely going to have sex, I needed uninterrupted yet protected time with the "D" and then I also needed space and time to think *by myself*.

Lemme' ask a question? Have you ever had makeup sex? If not, I feel bad for you. For those that have, imagine the kinda sex ya best guy would give if he knew you was two seconds from leaving his ass. The kinda sex that will make a man use FMLA to take you away just to beg you to stay. Yes, we had all of that and then some type of sex.

Every morning after my meditation, Corey would lean me over the banister on the balcony of my cabin and suck on my *honeypot* until my legs would shake. I would wake up to him under my blanket.

He was being so perfect, bringing small gifts every day, rub downs after my shower. I mean we ran thru two value packs of Magnums. Chile, it was everything, too bad it had to end.

I sure did take that much needed relaxation part of a messed-up situation and came back home *plotting*. *I was trying hard* find a way of escape.

My entire plane ride home I brainstormed, 'how Ima flee this dude' but then thank god for whoever's granddad prayed at the altar because Corey was the daddy to both those babies! Chile, word hit the streets the week we came back. Both babymoms could not wait to post pictures of the results. I was free...those babies broke us up.

'Still my peoples though', but now looking back, I don't feel bad about how I secured some things in my proceedings.

Oh Chile, yes this was *that ex*. *Proceedings, as in courts and 'Your honors'; just* a whole thing. Like I really almost went to prison for conspiracy to commit fraud.

They were laying out this life before my eyes. A life that seemed familiar, but I had no clue, so when the prosecutor asked, "So you had no idea" in several different ways. My answer was always the same.

I really sat there looking like a complete ass. And I was okay with it because I genuinely had no idea.

But did you hear how I said, the *prosecutor* asked...yes honey! This turned into a thing, Sis thought she was outta here. I was nervous, I don't like chicks and I'm cute. I did not even feel like going to prison.

But when it was all said and done, Corey rocked out for me because although he had some shady real estate dealings, he said he really cared about me, so he told the truth. I was able to walk away free and clear.

During the trial, I had called my Uncle Sammy to show him the paperwork, he's the numbers guy, they all said. By the time he got through breaking down what legally could belong to me; between the businesses '*I invested in*' that turned profit and property value from businesses that my name was on that I knew *nothing* about. I had quite a few dollars to play with. I found all of that out the weekend *before* the last day of testimony. I was nineteen years old; Corey was twenty-five.

Of course, Corey swore he was trying to purchase the apartment and commercial property as a surprise for me. I mean, that's what he told me when I called him on speakerphone in the hallway; at my attorney's office after hours, giving my lawyer time to prepare documents.

The next day we presented a check for the balance to the bank for both properties and a request to transfer the deed into just my name.

And of course, we waited until after his testimony where Corey testified to my ignorance to his fraudulent activity. Corey let me walk away on top, so I had love for him. I had seen dudes sink chicks over less. And if he did feel some type of way then he never showed it.

After Corey came home from serving his time, he came by the building to as he called it, 'show his love and respect'. He dropped off a gift. A black Audi truck with black leather interior and tinted windows. I promised one back during our first time around.

"You got me a truck" I asked as I jogged down the stairs.

Corey apologized and asked could we work on being friends. He even offered a reference for contracting work for my renovations. "Well, I already did the big stuff but yeah. Thank you for the offer" I thanked him for his help.

Corey continued to come by and I entertained him against the objection from my family. I thought he was different, plus he looked out and protected me, right? I mean after all; I owned the first two floors in a six-story building that has a commercial set up on first floor with office space on the second floor. There are apartments on third and fourth and the previous owner renovated the fifth and sixth floors into a custom setup, that became my first apartment. I just used the rent from the commercial properties to pay for my expenses.

I did not know the whole while he's on a 'we can be *friends first* campaign' this bastard was making two whole families on me.

So, after what I went through with him, then Logan and now I'm learning more things about Rafiq. I really don't know if I'm up for another bullshit ass relationship. But there is something about my new thang, he's very new so we'll see.

Damn I keep bouncing all over the place...Ok so let us recap, I flew out of town to get my mind off Corey and all that folly.

That's right, I'm supposed to be explaining how I met Logan...

Chapter 3: Logan

'I'm the Baby Murphy...'

I sat in that airport hungover, high, sleepy and very irritated. This is the last time I let LeRoy, my oldest brother, book my ticket. I had a two hour and forty-five-minute layover, definitely would not have booked this flight because I don't do layovers, I hate 'em!

I looked at my watch as I put my phone in my hoodie pocket while walking to the next gate. I'm already annoyed at my older brother LeRoy aka Boy aka Mr. Who Gives a fuck, for not choosing my seat *and* for putting me in coach, but whatever…

I'm not about to lose it, I'm way too tired. I barely slept all weekend. I'm just gonna find me a bar, have a drink and order me some wings.

As I walked over to a bar type setup, I looked over and saw this girl walking over to the counter to order.

Oh shit, it's her!

I walked behind *her* towards the main door. She was on the phone as she walked into the bar, "I can order food at the bar, right?" she asked as she pulled out a stool.

After seeing her getting the head nod from the bartender. I opted to sit at the bar as well, but further down to see the game on TV. I had seen this girl at this party two night ago. She smelled and looked good enough to eat.

I played around on my phone as I waited for my food. They were starting to board, according to my message notification. I figure since I'm in the damn trunk of the plane, I had time to eat my food before they close the doors. Throughout my meal, I would check to see if she was still at the bar, and she was but this time I looked down the bar, she was gone.

'Damn, maybe she's at one of the gates close to mine' I thought.

I looked down the corridor, but I didn't even see her walking.

I paid my tab and began heading towards the gate. I walked down the corridor to board the plane, I stepped inside and saw *her* sitting in first class looking through her purse. *She* looked up at me and I smiled.

Now, I'm not exactly sure of the type smile I gave her, but I didn't feel like it was a cool dude type smile. Let's just say I felt like a real young boy when she brushed off my smile and looked back into her bag. I just put my head down and walked to my seat.

I looked back and caught her checking me out. But the further I walked to the back of the plane, the more I hoped she wasn't still watching me.

'There's no way I'm staying back here, there has to be an empty seat in first class' I thought to myself.

I waited for the doors to close before I called over a stewardess. It took some work, but I finally made it to first class sitting right behind *her. Then, after* paying a guy fifty bucks, mission accomplished! I was finally in the seat next to *her*.

We began making small talk, her name is MaJhonnie, but she prefers to be called Jhonnie. By the end of our flight, I learned she was friends with Neesh, one of our homegirls.

"You do look familiar" she said as she sipped her drink.

She had just turned twenty-three and had graduated from a Master's program and she lives in Overville aka Da Ville, which was about thirty, maybe forty minutes across the bridge from me in heavy traffic. She was close enough. Jhonnie was a smart ass but you can tell she was cool.

I was going to ask her for her number when we landed once she turned on her phone, but as soon as it powered on it began ringing.

I heard her talking, "Ok yeah I'll be home in like an hour. Awww, love you too" then she did this giggle that changed my mind.

The stewardess rolled my carry-on to the front and smiled as she thanked me for flying. I grabbed my bag and told Jhonnie it was nice meeting her. I walked off the plane heading to the exit.

I called my brother Boy, he started explaining without saying hello, "I'm circling back around now, Lo" he said ending the call.

I slid my hoodie over my head and walked down the escalator. I put the phone in my pocket as I walked through the doors to go outside. I was standing out front waiting for Boy when Jhonnie came out the doors wheeling her bag. She walked across the street and stood next to me.

"Somebody's in a rush" she cut her eyes over at me smirking.

I shook my head, "Not even, I just hate airports and people" I moved off the post gesturing for her to use it to lean against since there weren't any seats.

"Awww, thank you" she walked over and propped herself against the post.

Boy pulled up and honked the horn. I turned around and gave him 'the middle finger' and with my eyes wide as hell, I mouthed, 'Da fuck is you doin'

Boy threw his hands up as if to apologize.

I turned back around to Jhonnie, "Is that your ride?" she asked.

I flagged my hand in my brother's direction, "Yeah my brother, but um *you good?"* I asked.

Jhonnie glanced at her phone. "Yeah, my car should have been here. I ordered another one just now."

I backed up towards the truck, "Ight, well you be cool" I turned to walk away.

She called out. "Ey"

I turned around feeling kinda disrespected. *'Now I see how girls feel' I thought as I walked back over to her.*

"Word, 'Ey" I repeated.

She smirked as she put her hands in her pockets. "I figured you didn't want me yelling your name all out in the public" she replied.

I gave her a head nod and put my hands in my front hoodie pocket. "So, what's up?" I asked.

She looked to the side. "You wouldn't happen to have more of whatever you smoked before you got on our flight, would you?" she asked in a weirdo tone.

I cut my eyes at her. She is either a true-life smoker or sis is a narc. Yea, I smoked! I smoked with Bop *before* I left for the airport *but that was before* I took a shower and got dressed.

She held her hand up, "Relax, I'm no cop! I smelled it, it's probably on your coat or maybe in your hat" I looked up at my cap.

I shook my head sticking with my latter feelings. "Nah, sorry but it's plenty boys in ya town that could help you out" I backed up walking towards the truck.

I put my hood on my head as I lifted my bag into the truck. "Yo Boy" I hugged my brother as I climbed inside.

"She's pretty" Boy mentioned as he pulled into traffic.

"Nah, something didn't feel right! But anyway, where's Mr. *Tucker?*" I asked.

LeRoy glanced over. "Where you think?" he asked.

I looked up from my phone. 'Yo this guy' I scrolled to his name and pressed the *call* button. "Ayo, he sent me to 'fuck you'" I chuckled.

Boy started laughing. "You know how ole *'Tuck her'* do Baby! He a lover not a runner" he joked.

I leaned back in the seat, "Oh yeah speaking of running numbers, you owe me three hundred dollars" I said which made him blow raspberries.

"I can't wait to hear this; how do I owe you...how much you said?" he asked.

I sat up in my seat and lifted my feet, "three hundred dollars" I flopped back down and fixed my hat. "That's how much it cost me to sit in first class with that fucking narc" I said pointing behind me.

LeRoy looked in his mirror as he switched lanes.

"Boy, ain't nobody behind us. I don't know if she really is a narc, but she asked me about buying weed talking bout she smelled it on me, he hit me with 'maybe it's your hat' shit" I mimicked what she said.

LeRoy took my hat. "You wore this hat all weekend didn't you" he nodded his head.

I snatched it out his hand to inspect it. "Yeah, I don't smell anything" fanning the hat in front of my nose.

Boy looked at me in disbelief, "Lo, are you kidding me? I sniffed the hat and I'm high" he said jokingly.

I took my hat off again, "Say word" I smelled it again,

Boy looked in the mirror again. "It's resonating in the truck at this point" he cracked all the windows.

"Pu- I mean Pop wants to know if you coming to this brunch thing on Sunday" Boy asked as he switched lanes.

I nodded my head. "Hold on, I'm thinking, I messed up, didn't I? Me on my shit thought baby girl was being shady, ugghhh" I yelled.

I fell back into my seat. Kicking myself considering the missed opportunity. "Naw like she cute as shit, I definitely liked her. I paid three hundred to sit next to her, feel me? But I just kept getting this weird vibe" I looked over at my brother, he looked over at me.

"So, is that a *no to brunch? I gotta* give Pop an answer, are you going?" he asked.

LeRoy obviously was ignoring my plight as he repeats the question about Sunday. "Boy, why are you even asking me that dumb shit, don't I go to *everything.*" I asked.

He nodded his head and agreed. "Yeah, you do".

Boy tapped back into my conversation, "Ok, so back to ole girl, is she from here or was she just visiting?"

I looked over at Boy, "Who visits Da 'Ville" I laughed as he pulled onto our other brother Leviathan's street.

Me and Leviathan are twenty months apart, people think we're twins. We call him Levi, Lee or as of recent courtesy of Roy da Boy, he's Tuck-her, or Tucker.

Tucker came about because Levi started to disappear for days with some girl that he's *been* creeping with for months and we would never see that shit coming, until his ex-Tina had enough and she decided to make a scene, which would always set Levi's quiet ass off.

"Have you ever seen crazy parked" I pointed at Tina sitting in a car up the street.

LeRoy waved at her. I knocked on the door and waited before I tapped again.

"Lo, dontchu have a key" Leroy asked.

I held up a finger before the alarm deactivated and I unlocked the door.

"He got company, why you think Dirty Diana parked up the block?" I laughed.

LeRoy stepped back to look up the block. "And she still there too, she ain't even try to circle the block or nothing, when she saw us" he joked.

"Nah, that's ole shit, she doesn't hide no more, she'll stay there until he come out with whoever, you'll see. Lee 'bout to be out here snapping" I said as I locked the door.

LeRoy shook his head in disbelief, "Not Lee" he retorted.

"If I didn't see it myself, I'd have the same reaction Boy" I climbed the stairs towards his room.

Levi was our more super chill brother; it took a lot to get him going. But once he gets going...it can get crazy, real quick.

I remember one day his neighbor Ms Jessie, an older lady from across the street, waved me over. "How you doin' Ms Jessie?" I asked as I stood in her driveway as she closed her trunk.

"Tell Leviathan I shooed that girl from round here the other week".

Ms Jessie's the one that told me about Tina parking on the block just watching his house.

I already know he's about to hit the sky real fast when I tell him about Tina being outside again. Especially now, he ain't feeling Tina, she did some real dumb shit.

I knocked on his room door, "It's me and Boy whenever you're ready! Oh, and that problem Ms Aunt Jessie had…"

I waited for his response. "Well, it's back, we out here" I tapped the door and walked back downstairs.

I was looking at my phone when Boy snapped his finger to get my attention, "Did you just snap at me?" I asked without looking at him.

Boy waved his arms in the air. "Why are you so loud? Go head, finish telling me bout Levi and you know ole girl, Dirty Diana" LeRoy whispered

I shook my head. "I'm not gon have too, just watch what happen" I said pushing off the counter.

I walked inside the kitchen as Levi came downstairs with his company. I cut through into the dining room to get a good seat at the window.

Boy walked over and stood next to me. We saw Levi walk a baddy to a white with tinted windowed Mercedes.

"Okay Tuck, I see you baby" Roy said as Levi sent her home with his infamous self-titled 'givin'em something to think about' type kiss.

"Look at her, she doesn't want to leave" Boy joked, "You think she gon join Tina's stakeout when this is all over because *we know* Tuck don't keep 'em too long?" LeRoy joked and I laughed at the thought and possibilities of it all.

"Look, oh shit" I pointed.

As soon as the girl pulled off, Tina pulled up and the fight broke out. They were going back and forth. Levi would walk away then go back yelling.

"Yo, Lee talking to her like he's ready to hit her" he said.

I cut my eyes over at Roy. "I'm surprised he hasn't, Tina did some fucked up shit to Lee" I shared

"Oh, I know, I heard" Roy nodded his head.

Levi kicked Tina's car and she sped off.

I hurried back into the kitchen as he walked back inside.

"And fuck you two drawin' asses for sitting in the goddam window" Levi said throwing his phone on the counter.

I could tell by the scowl on his face and his heavy breathing, he was still trying to come down. I didn't even bother trying to engage him, of course Boy didn't share my way of thinking, so he kept pressing Lee with questions and he almost saw Leviathan Murphy on twenty.

"So Lee, what's going on?" Boy asked.

Levi looked over at me and I shook my head to signal for him to relax. Levi opened the fridge, "Nothing Boy, I got it" he drank his water.

Boy kept on with his questions. Levi walked over to the table and put his drink down. "How 'bout I'll start answering questions about who I'm doin' and shit, when you answer those *same* questions Big Dawg" Levi said as he tapped the table while looking LeRoy in the eyes.

I hit the counter in agreement, "*Hell yeah*, at least Levi don't just pop up with kids and have chicks fighting each other at ya other kid's parties but steady claiming he *'ain't got a girl...yeah, at least Lee ain't doing nothing like that"* I said.

I shared that tidbit to help my brother get our other brother up off him.

Levi extended his fist for a dab, "My Man" he said.

"You *already know*" I replied.

Boy held his hands up in defeat, "Alright fair enough, I'll mind my business" he opened his water. "But I do have *one more* question" we both looked over at him. "I thought you and Tina had an 'understanding" Boy asked.

Levi shook his head. "We did until she moved in with her dude" Levi shared before he grabbed his keys. "We ridin or not" Levi asked as he walked towards the door.

We rolled through town checking on things. "Yo Lee, you used to hang over in Da Ville; you ever heard of a girl named MaJhonnie?" I asked.

He thought for a second then shook his head. "Not that I can recall" Levi looked up. "Why who is she?" he asked.

Roy looked in the rearview mirror. "Just a girl your brother met in the airport" he advised.

Levi put his phone up to his ear. "Yo Dumps, you know some girl named MaJhonnie" Levi tapped my shoulder and gave a thumbs up.

"That's her cousin? Okay cool" Levi ended the call.

"She's way outta ya league Lo" Levi smiled as he leaned on the armrest in the middle of the backseat.

"Fuck you mean, she's outta my league" I turned around to look at my brother.

He smiled, "She's not into that whole street life vibe" Levi said as he put his phone back to his ear.

"Yo Jay, what's up man" he began his inquiry into MaJhonnie from Da Ville.

I turned to Boy. "Ima slap the shit out ya brother" I said calmly.

Levi laughed then I heard my phone chime. I looked at the message then at Levi.

"How the hell" I said in disbelief

I looked at my screen. I was staring at a contact for "Jhonny"

I turned to Levi, "Do your thing" he said then nodded his head as he kept talking on the phone.

"I'm damn sure not calling her around y'all" I put the phone back in my pocket.

My brothers had me out all night. I walked into the house with the sun. I'll call her another day.

The next week I was coming out of the dry cleaners for my grandmom when I saw her again.

"Ey" I turned and saw MaJhonnie walking across the street.

"Here you go with that 'Ey' shit…" I replied.

She smiled. "How are you" she asked walking past me towards a shiny building.

"I've been cool" I replied.

Jhonnie walked up to a door but I grabbed the handle to pull it open for her. "Listen, can I call you sometime?" I asked.

She reached in her bag and pulled out a square. She flipped it open and pulled out a business card, "I'm on vacation next week, so just call my cell, it's on there" Jhonnie said with a smile.

She walked into her building and I continued with my errands. I looked at her number on the card as I sat in the car.

"MaJhonnie Demby, Senior Consultant" I shrugged as I threw it into my cupholder and pulled into traffic heading to my brother's spot.

Levi walked down the stairs as I closed the front door. "My man" he said as he hugged me before walking into the kitchen.

"Guess who I saw when I was running errands for Mi-Mi" I said following behind him.

Levi slapped his forehead. "Oh, shit Lo, was she mad? I was supposed to do that for her" he said.

"Naw, I told her I would do it, but she couldn't come" I shook my head.

Levi laughed, "Yeah, that's smart because she will add extra trips and have you way out somewhere for the *entire* day" he joked.

I agreed with him as I slid his package across the table. "Yeah, she will, but back to who I saw" I lit the el and pulled on it.

"The girl Jhonnie, right?" he asked.

I looked at Levi like he was crazy. "How the hell you know that" I asked him.

Levi laughed. "I found out when I got her number for you, she works close to Mi-Mi's dry cleaners and favorite bakery. The goal was for me to see her because I thought you would have been called her, but hey..." he said walking over to the trash, tossing some things inside.

"So, what's up with her" Levi asked as he leaned over on his elbows.

"She looked *better* than I remembered" I said.

I walked past Levi to sit down at the table. I nodded at him and he took the *el* from me.

"*Sooo, what's up with her?*" Levi repeated with a chuckle as he pulled out a chair across from me at the table.

"I don't know, she said she's on vacation next week and to call her cell" I held up her card.

Levi took the card out of my hand.

"Senior Consultant" he frowned his face, "See man, this is what I meant when I said *outta ya league*, I'm not sure if you're ready for an intelligent babe" Levi laughed.

"Listen brotha, I'm about to be twenty-one soon. I can't do this playa shit forever" I rebutted.

Levi smirked at me repeating the same conversation he brought to me two years ago when he turned twenty-one. Since that time, to be honest, Levi has slowed down forreal. Even in the streets, he only come out with me or Roy Boy *if* we legit needed him to ride.

When Levi stepped back, he introduced me to some influential people. I can't front, I kinda liked being the baby regarding my family's connections. I'm at the end of a long line of powerful men. I can be a savage asshole but only on the strength of being tried. Yes, I'm the baby but I'm very protective of my older brothers.

LeRoy, the eldest, he's now what we call an OG out here. He has a few businesses under his belt, and he has a tight crew. They hold down our old hood. I fucked around and fell into some premium exotic smoke so now Roy and my brother's buy from me for themselves, as well as *their folks*. *I don't work directly with and I don't touch,* so I live a quiet life.

Then there's Lance aka Pudd or Pop, when talking to Boy.

He's the underground connection for anything we need done "off the books" as we call it, which amongst us really just means "without Roy da Boy knowing" we went to Pudd.

Pudd became known as the 'bid' brother, early in the game. He went in and out of the county jail with no problem, mostly for assaults. I think it was after his second prison stay, he came home and didn't even fake it, he went with what he knew, which was illegal living and it worked out for him. He's the second to the oldest out of the Murphy Brother's.

It was something else that happened on the last stay. Pudd came home and the streets were talking crazy shit about my brother. It wasn't my story to discuss, so I waited for him to bring it to me. When Pudd confirmed to me and Levi the rumors were true he first asked us to hear his side. I remember the night we sat at his house listening to his horror story of the things he had to do and endure while being locked up over the years.

Levi wiped his wet face and took a deep breath, but I spoke first, "I mean, I can't even begin to tell you where my mind would have gone if that shit happened to me" I joked but had never been more serious. "I'm not going *that* far but they definitely gon suffer!"

Pudd nodded in agreement, "And that they did" he nodded.

Then there's Leviathan, my goal is be like Levi, he just be down to invest his money and live off profits. He moves around like that; no real worries and I like that shit.to

Now I'm not gonna act like our family is some big-time cartel. Not even, our level-up money came from our mother's death. My mother spent most of me and Levi's young life in prison. But somehow, my mother knew enough to have a life insurance policy for two million dollars, split amongst my brothers and our Dad.

We all invested it in one way or another to make more money. My pops went heavy into real estate. He still tries to push us to do his real estate investments full-time.

Me and Levi are his silent partners in his company. We don't like the meetings but we definitely like those random deposits every couple months or so, for tens of thousands of dollars. That just recently started though, even still, I have no real complaints. I just move out here and try to live my life.

Out of the four of us, Levi and I are the closest. We don't live too far from each other and because of our ages, we always had been together.

Levi closed the refrigerator, "Ayo, so Pops wants to know where you want your birthday party?" he asked.

I looked at Levi making pancake batter. "Make me some" he nodded. "Umm, that place where Pudd had his wedding" I smiled.

Levi looked over at me and died laughing. "Don't start your shit" Levi said wiping up the mess he made during his laughing episode.

"You know damn well; we can't go nowhere near that place, right?" he laughed again.

"Naw I'm playing, wherever, I'm not even thinking about my party right now" I said unconvincingly.

Levi looked at me then twisted his lips.

"Ok maybe a little, I wanna be on some grown and sexy casino type shit with a bad one on my arm" I said cheesing at the thought.

Levi nodded his head and kept cooking, "So is your scary ass gon call the girl Jhonnie or what" Levi asked as I looked at the card again.

I put the card face down on the table. "I don't want to just call her, I kinda wanted her to call me" I told my brother my reasoning.

Levi looked over at me, "How is she supposed to do that when she doesn't have your number?" he asked.

"Huh, dickhead? You tryna figure that part out, right?" he said shaking his head.

I leaned back in my chair. "That's where you come in help me out, gimme some of those good ole Tucker moves" I said hitting the counter.

Levi grabbed the hand towel off the counter and starting humming as he thought, "Find out her favorite lunch spot and send her lunch with a note, have Pudd make her something and deliver it, you already know she's a smoker. *Or* just man up, call her and invite her to hang out" he offered as he flagged his hands in the air.

"No, Ima call her let it ring then hang up. That way, she'll call me back" I laughed picking up my phone. I let the phone ring twice, and as I went to end the call she answered.

"Hey MaJhonnie? This is Logan, um I know you're probably busy so I was just calling to give you my number so you can call when you can talk" I said.

Levi was twirling a hand towel in the air. I got up from the table and walked into the living room.

"No, it's cool, what's up?" she said clearing her throat.

I sat down on the couch. Levi brought my plate over to me and walked away. It wasn't until he walked back in fully dressed that I realized I had been talking on the phone for over an hour.

"My bad, I gotta make a run with my brother real quick, call me when you get home" I ended the call.

Levi smiled. "I don't want to hear no more jokes about me being a telephone lover" he said taking my hand to pull me up off the couch.

I nodded my head as we walked outside. "Well, I found out all the information to do some of that shit you suggested earlier" I advised my brother.

Levi laughed, "Aww is 'the baby' growing up" Levi teased as he backed out of his driveway.

He backed up to talk to Ms Aunt Jessie working in her yard. "Hey Ms Auntie" he sang out the window and she lit up.

"Hey there boys, I got my eyes out" we both laughed.

"I'm going to bring your cake tomorrow" Levi leaned across me and yelled, she gave a thumbs up and we pulled off.

"Cake, what cake" I asked rolling the window back up.

"The ones your brother makes" he replied with a grin.

I don't think I've ever laughed so hard. "Get the fuck outta here, Ms Ant Jessie get on" I clapped my hands and went into another round of laughter.

"She got a whole little squad, she's his biggest plug for the aunties" he said jokingly.

I looked at Levi. "That's what's up, I knew I liked her" I laughed.

My phone chimed, I looked at the message. I took a deep breath, "Now here go Shamira" I said putting the phone down.

Levi looked at me. "Talkin' shit like that's not *your* Tina" he pulled into Roy's development.

"I have a feeling Jhonnie would give Shamira a run though, she looks like she don't play *no games*" I shared.

I smiled as Boy got into the car. I ignored Shamira's messages, "Ima try to keep Jhonnie away from her until you know..."

I slid my hand across the air, "...things smooth out" I laughed.

Levi nodded. "Smart man" he laid back in his seat.

Yeah, *real smart man*. Fast forward two months to my casino party and all my folks are in town. My brothers all wore black suits with black shirts. Mine was white on black. I felt great and felt even better when Jhonnie said she'd be my date. I was excited that she was gon be on my arm. My party would be our debut. We had been kickin' it and she was mad cool.

Everyone was excited to meet Jhonnie, even Mi-Mi. It blew my mind when I heard her and my grandmom talk on the phone. My Pops walked over and started fixing my tie.

"You're looking very dapper son" he hugged me. "Where's your lady friend I'm hearing so much about" he stood next to me with his arm around my shoulders.

I scanned the room, "She just walked in" I smiled as I drank the last of my drink. "I'll be right back" I dapped him and walked across the room.

MaJhonnie looked beautiful. She smiled as I walked over towards her. "Thank you for coming" I kissed her hand as she introduced her two friends Rebecca and Amira.

I knew Amira, she used to work at the juvenile place my brother was locked up in before. "Hi Logan" she smiled at me.

"Whatchu working?" Pudd asked smiling.

Amira smiled and embraced Pudd as he walked over, "Hi Lance, how have you been" Amira waved as she winked at Boy.

I could not believe he started blushing. I made a note to myself to bring that up later with the fellas...

I turned my attention back to Jhonnie. "Would you like a drink" I held out my arm to escort her to our area, we had just given our orders when Levi walked over and whispered in my ear.

"Pops want to talk with us real quick" he pointed to the back.

I showed Jhonnie to our section that overlooked the dance floor. "I'll be right back, it's food over there and there's three bars over there. Order whatever you want" I followed Levi to the backroom.

"What's up Pop" I walked into the room.

He was sitting at the table, "What all do you know about your lady friend" he stood up.

I shrugged my shoulders as I looked over at Levi. "I know enough, she's cool. I know one thing, she ain't making it easy for the kid" I joked.

Levi chuckled at me. I had told him about her ninety-day rule, which hopefully ends after tonight.

"Where's she from? Who's her people?" he asked.

I shrugged then remembered her mother's name was Celeste. "Her pops died a lil while ago, but her mom's name is um...Celeste" I said.

My father sat down, then stood up to embrace Roy as he walked into the room.

"Celeste from Da Ville?" he asked.

I nodded as I looked at Levi. We knew our dad had some bones in those streets but never cared to inquire.

Roy sat at the table, "Who's Celeste, one of your old babes Pop?" he asked.

He looked at Roy and shrugged. "Once upon a time son, once upon a time. What was her Daddy's name?" he asked.

I looked at my father and shook my head. "Her father passed away like a year or so ago" I answered.

He put his cigar back into his mouth and turned to the window.

Just then Pudd popped into the room. "Ey Lo, Shamira in the VIP looking for trouble and I think she found it" we all ran out the room.

"Oh, come on" I said as I walked into the VIP to see Jhonnie with her forearm up to Shamira's neck as her home girls blocked Shamira's girls from getting to Jhonnie.

I walked over, "Jhonnie, it's cool" I said as Levi took Jhonnie's hands and walked her away.

Boy and I escorted Shamira and her friends down to the ground floor.

"Fuck you Lo, so is that why you're ignoring your son" everybody including me repeated after Shamira.

"*Son*" I laughed at her using *her* son like a pawn.

"You know damn well we don't have any kids together, go home! I'm good" I flagged my hand in her direction.

I turned her by her shoulders, then called out to my brother, from another Bop. "Yo Bop, she's not welcomed anymore" he nodded then had his female security escort her outside of the party.

When I walked back to our section. Levi told me Jhonnie left. "Fuck" I smacked the napkins off the table.

Levi grabbed me and shook me as he handed me a glass.

"Don't worry about that shit, this is your day" he said handing me a glass.

I decided he was right, I'll deal with this shit tomorrow...or the day after, I drank a little too much at my party and was what we called "in da cooker" for at least two days.

Levi and Roy came to my spot. "Lo" I heard Levi call my name as I stepped out of the bathroom.

"My man, what's good Boy" I shook their hands as I sipped my Gatorade.

"You talk to Pop" Levi asked

I shook my head. "Not since the party, I haven't called anybody not even Jhonnie. She's been calling like crazy; I know she's mad as shit, I'll call her later" I sipped my drink then screwed the top back on.

"Why what's up?" I asked.

Levi looked at me then at Boy, "What" I asked picking up on their weirdo vibes.

Boy leaned onto the counter. "You don't remember do you" he asked.

I looked at them confused. "You don't remember Pop telling us he thinks MaJhonnie could be our sister?" he asked.

I dropped the bottle onto the floor. *Thank God the top was on. Damn I guess I drank way more than I thought.*

"Our sister" I repeated.

Levi pulled out a chair. "Pop admitted he did have an affair on mom, but the only issue is, according to Pop he ain't sleep with Celeste" Levi said.

I looked at Levi real confused. He continued, "He was messing with some married lady named Safia, Sophie; or something like that. But she was from down Warrinton but ran the streets in da 'Ville" he finished.

I shrugged. "Well then she's not our sister because Jhonnie's mom's name is Celeste" I offered as justification.

Levi nodded his head. "I know but Pop's is saying Jhonnie looks just like this *Sa-phia* lady" Levi said.

I looked at Levi and he could tell I was visibly annoyed.

"So, what *all* is he saying" I asked looking over at Boy and he immediately looked at the ground.

"Pop asked that until he is sure that you lay low with Jhonnie" he said then took a deep breath.

I looked at my brothers. "So, let me get this straight, I meet a girl that's perfect for me and just when shit is going good, you're telling me she could be my *sister?"* I asked in disbelief.

I hit the counter and walked away.

Thinking back, I guess it was a lot of good things that came out of me meeting Jhonnie. Not only did we find our sister, but we also reconnected them, our father and Sofiya. Sofiya told us initially she did not believe it because supposedly her baby died at birth, until Jhonnie popped back up with her godson.

He was supposedly back in love with a girl named Jhonnie, from Da Ville. I found all of this out during the months I had to avoid Jhonnie.

It had been over a few weeks since the party, "This shit is getting real deep Lee" I said walking past my brother from another, Bop as he was standing at the stove.

"Lemme get one! And I want mine just as *fancy as yours*" " I pointed to Bop.

Levi laughed as he joked about coming over to get 'one of Bop's fancy for no reason sandwiches.'

"So yeah, I guess when y'all figure it out let me know in the meantime I'll keep feeling like a piece of shit" I shared my feelings with them.

Levi looked at me confused. "She's calling me, and I can't answer because I'll just tell her straight up like, 'I think you're my sister and your dead Dad might notta been ya pops after all" I raised my hands.

Bop and Levi shared how serious they were that even if I did tell Jhonnie, I had to swear I would not tell her that way.

"So, word is she's like the best friend turned on/off thing with some dude they call Ski from down on the Southside" I said.

Bop dropped the spoon on the floor. "Lee, lemme go so I can keep my eyes on Bop. I swear he was about to put that spoon back in the Kool-Aid; if I wasn't sitting here" I joked.

Levi laughed and ended the call.

"Everything Alright" I leaned over the counter looking at Bop looking under the sink.

"Yeah, I'm cool" Bop said as he stood up and washed off the silverware.

"You coming to Pudd's on Sunday right" I asked looking at my ringing phone.

Bop nodded his head, "Oh most definitely" he replied as I picked up my plate and walked into the tv room.

Chapter 4: Jhonnie

'I call him Ole Faithful...'

Not too long after I graduated from college, my cousin Brandi moved South, so she was living between two spots, she had been trying for months to get me to come visit. Finally, she convinced me to come on a long weekend visit, she finally closed on her house.

"Yes, I bought the ticket" I said into the phone for the eightieth time.

Brandi's housewarming in her new town meant a lot to her so I absolutely had to be there.

"I'm coming" I said.

I sat on the bed and sorted through some shirts I planned to pack. Brandi was steady threatening what she would do to me if I missed my flight.

"Rebecca taking you to the airport?" she asked.

"No, I'm not telling nobody I'm leaving, not even Rhyon." I shared.

I hopped off the bed to get my small suitcase out the closet in my spare room. I rolled the bag back in the room and began packing.

"Stink, you are a mess, your flight leaves in five hours and you're just now packing" Brandi said in between her chewing whatever she was eating loudly in my ear.

"Oh my god Bessie" I said annoyed.

She laughed at me. "Shut up, call me when you get to the airport, so I know you didn't miss your flight" Brandi said before ending the call.

To *everyone's* surprise, I always make it to the airport on time. My Aunt Dell called me, "Whatchu doing up?" she asked over my music.

I explained I was packing for my flight. I barely finished my statement before my aunt started in on me.

I did not have the heart to tell my aunt that because I was already TSA pre-approved and bringing a carryon, I didn't need to go through all those lines. Plus, I did not want to have to explain what it was or how TSA worked. So, I just listened to her tell me 'how my life was going to be forever chaotic because I have terrible time management skills, which according to my aunt dates back to '*ever since I was little...*'

She must be mad at my mom, that is usually when my aunt points out the flaws in my life.

I was walking through the airport when I saw Brandi standing at the bottom of the escalator. After we hugged, I made jokes about her 'slow town' downgrade from our fast city living.

Brandi deactivated the alarm on a shiny black two door BMW car.

"Oh, is *that* how you felt" I asked with my eyebrows raised.

Brandi laughed as she climbed in the car. "You know, a lil something" she put on her shades as she pulled into traffic.

She looked at my hair, "I love your doo, that cut is cute. I didn't think you'd go that short though." She commented on my drastic change from mid back to short bob.

I touched my soft waves and pin curls. "Yeah, trying something new" I said.

We pulled up to her rancher style home that sat on a half-acre of land.

My mouth dropped as Brandi pulled around and I saw a two-story deck with a winding staircase connecting the house in the back. It made the house look chic. Brandi's house sat on a hill, but it didn't appear so from the front. "It's two stories, I love it" I climbed out the car and grabbed my bag.

Brandi gave me the tour and we laughed about the corny neighbor turned sexy after hearing he was a surgeon. "Girl please, you don't like good boys" she joked as she walked into the closet.

"I tried a 'good boy' or so I thought and looked what happened to me, was almost locked down somewhere singing, Roxanne" I pushed down the memory of my crazy ex.

Brandi chuckled, "Not Roxanne!?! Well, hopefully you'll like it so much here that you'll stay" Brandi walked out of the closet.

"I'm working on Birry" she smiled widely.

Birry is her sister-friend Kabira that has been very verbal in her refusal to make the move. Especially since Rhyon our other cousin, her now boyfriend already said he's not leaving his space of the world.

"So, what exactly are we doing?" I asked.

Brandi plopped down on her bed. "This guy from my company invited me to his friend's business launch party tonight. Tomorrow, I am speaking at a brunch. You're more than welcome to come" she smiled.

I nodded my head. "Absolutely, what else am I doing?" I adjusted my shirt.

She snapped her fingers. "And then Sunday is *my* day" I clapped my hands as I got up off the bed.

"Well let me get a nap" I grabbed my bag and pointed looking around for directions to my space.

"Out the door, across the hall and go one door down to your right" she directed.

I rolled my bag into the room and opened the blanket folded across the bottom of the bed. In no minutes, I was sleep. I stayed up all night packing and cleaning my house, with plans to sleep on the plan but that didn't happen, somebody baby was crying thee entire flight.

It also did not help that her mattresses felt like fluffy marshmallows, just a phenomenal amount of comfort. I don't even remember much after my head hit the pillow.

I woke up to a light tap on my door. Brandi peeked her head in the room. "Ma'am, are you planning on going out tonight?" she asked sarcastically.

I rolled over and looked at my phone on the charger. 'Seven thirty' I dropped the phone on the bed.

"My bad" I kicked the blanket back.

"I see you tied that head up this time" Brandi joked as she cut the lights up and turned the house on.

I threw my robe on and walked across the hall to her room.

"What type of shin dig is this? Will there be seating? Is it indoor/outdoor? I mean I'm prepared for anything just need to know" I tied a bow in my belt and leaned against the door frame.

Brandi looked at me, "Did you make that?" she asked pointing to my emerald, green robe with a kimono type belt wrap.

I kicked my legs out to show my robe. "Yes, you like?" I asked.

She walked over to feel the material. "It's *so soft*" she continued inspecting my robe.

I waved my hand, bringing her back to reality. "Girl, what are you working at that place for, why dontchu just do your own thing" she pleaded with me.

I was still raw behind losing my job after that whole F.E.D.S thing. I had gone back to my old job at the courthouse to make ends meet.

"Is that what you're wearing" I asked changing the topic.

She nodded as she threw a pair of wide leg pants across her bed. I nodded and walked back into the room I was staying in to get ready.

Cute and comfortable, the best kinda combination. I searched through my bag and pieced together a nice, cute and comfortable outfit.

"Are we ready" Brandi asked as I sprayed on my perfume.

"Ooohh I like that look" she said.

I turned around and Brandi touched my blazer. "You can just put this in my closet when you take it off" she ordered in a serious tone.

I smiled as I slid into my camel-colored peep-toe wedged sandals.

"That must be the car" she looked at the notification on her phone. "Yeah, he's out front are you ready" she asked.

I popped on my earring and grabbed my clutch. "We out"

I adjusted myself then stomped loudly in place. "Gotta make sure everything falls right!" I waved my arms along my body.

"You're so freakin' extra" she laughed as we walked out of the house.

Her sexy surgeon of a neighbor smiled and waved as he threw a duffle bag in his trunk. "Evening Ladies"

Brandi turned and looked at me. "Ooooooo, he never speaks..."

I tapped her plump rear end. "Maybe he ain't see all that before." Brandi laughed as she climbed into the car.

We rode to the party in silence, both looking through our phones. Brandi broke the silence, by announcing she had plans to 'sleep with Terrence later tonight'.

I looked at my cousin, "First off, who the hell is *Terrence?*"

Brand blushed as she proceeded to tell me about Terrence.

"So basically, I'm about to be a third wheel" I looked over my glasses at her.

"Stink cut it out, you'll be fine it's a party I'm not leaving you hanging, but I *am* letting you know about tonight, *after* the party. So, if you hear me doing my thang..." she smiled as she winked.

I shook my head, "Ugh, and I forgot my earplugs too" I joked as we pulled up to the party.

Brandi and I walked up to the door and the guy announced a fifty-dollar cover charge.

Not for a "relaxed dress code" situation.

I looked at my cousin, "They can have two of these, I thought your friend invited us, I *don't* pay when I get invited out, especially to get *into* a club" I stuck up my middle finger at the building.

Brandi told me to shut up then pulled me into the line. I kept looking at the outside and the parking lot was *pretty* empty. Then I looked again because I swore, I just saw my work bestie walk into the building.

She ain't tell me she was traveling nowhere…well hell I ain't tell her I was traveling.

"I'm about to ask if I could look inside to see if I see my friend" the familiar voice said to her crew before tapping one of the girls that walked by from behind the table to ask a question.

"I'll be right back" I heard her say before she walked inside.

Brandi pulled out her phone, so I turned around and smiled at the girls standing in line behind me. The one girl was very nice as she engaged me in conversation. She shared this was a local celebrity hang out, then she introduced me to her friends. I heard a bunch of commotion then I heard my friend in rare sarcastic form as she walked over towards the line.

"*Amira!!*" I waved her over. What are you doing out here? What happened" I asked moving over as she stepped in line.

"This jerk got all mad because I walked inside and saw it was empty as hell, so he gon tell me I gotta go back and pay" she explained.

Before I could ask her *what the hell she was doin' down here* or introduce my cousin, I caught sight of the big bouncer walking towards us. Amira moved her bag under arm as she shifted her weight onto one leg.

"Ooo here he come too" I said over her shoulder as she turned and prepared herself for the fuss.

"And I'm ready for him too" she fired back.

"Listen, you just can't walk in places doing that. Now who did you ask if you could just walk in? Because *I'm on the doe*" he said pointing to himself.

Amira took a deep breath then looked at me, "Please, be nice" I requested knowing my friend to be a pistol.

"Ok, and I said I understood that the first time. You're yelling at the wrong one, your co-worker or whoever she is let me walk inside when obviously you weren't *'on the doe"* Amira said while she pointed her finger in his direction.

I turned around to see an entourage of dudes that looked to be athletes walking towards the door.

That guy looked like Fiki! I said to myself trying to get a better look.

Fiki or Rafiq was my childhood friend that I would spend every summer with when I would visit my family until Rafiq moved right after senior year of high school.

I hadn't spoken to Rafiq in years, but I did reach out when I heard about his father being murdered when I was away at college. We tried a relationship, it flopped, that collab went nowhere far and I hadn't seen him since. But before that time, Rafiq had been my go-to guy. I didn't take him too seriously, I learned, Rafiq has a problem, he is "too cute for his own good".

Last I heard he was in fact, messing with some girl named, Karen and I fell all the way back from him. I didn't like the fact that he lied about her.

Amira kept arguing with the bouncer until her friend finally came outside to try and de-escalate the situation.

"Whoa, whoa whoa! I got this" he said waving his hands between Amira and the bouncer.

The friend quickly intervened and brought the matter under control. The guy moved the rope and took Amira's hand, she grabbed me all the while still shit talking' the bouncer. I quickly grabbed Brandi and dragged her inside.

After making introductions, Brandi shared she was going to look for her friends.

We walked inside and I had to admit it was a cute vibe, even better now because it was FREE. I walked over towards the coat check and handed her my blazer, "Thank you" I said as she gave me a ticket.

"Ooo girl this jacket is super cute" she said spinning it around looking at it on the hanger.

"You know what that's ok, thank you though. Oh no, you can keep it" I rejected my money back.

Amira touched my arm. "What's wrong?" she asked.

I turned to walk away. "Girl, the last time my coat was admired that hard at a coat check, I never saw it again" I folded the jacket and threw it over my arm as Amira handed me a drink.

"Girl, what are you working for" Amira asked for the thousandth time since I was fired from my job running a design company and I took a consultant position back with my old job in the judiciary building.

Oh yeah, that also happened while I was fighting for my freedom. I was an Executive at a Design Agency. I was trying to keep my job out of it, for as long as I could. I almost pulled it off *until* someone "anonymously" let the cat out of the bag to my CEO. But that's a whole 'notha story.

"I don't know" I shrugged not wanting to be *that serious* girl in the club. "Can we not, I'm tryna get my 'Party Bob' on" I danced in place.

Amira introduced me to her friend, that led us to another area with seating. I was standing in front of the couch but behind a table dancing to the music when I thought I heard someone call my name. Not my government, my family name, but when I looked around, I didn't see anything, so I blew it off.

I kept talking to Amira and a few of her new friends. Brandi came back over, and we danced for a couple songs.

The party was live, I enjoyed myself. I even met a couple cool dudes; it was a real chill night.

Brandi and I were walking to the car when I felt someone grab my hand pulling me back. I turned to look but was quickly spun around in a circle then pinned against an SUV.

Wait a minute? Is he smelling? Did he just kiss my neck? Why am I not stopping it? Wait...HOLD ON!

I pushed the person off of me trying to gather myself, then I focused my eyes on *him*.

"Fiki, I thought that was you!" I screamed.

I jumped on him and he hugged me. He squeezed me and I could not front that shit felt good. He put me back down then he kissed my cheek.

"You look good as shit! Whatchu doing out here?" he asked.

I looked around and grabbed Brandi's hand. "My cousin moved out here, so I came to visit her" I shared.

Rafiq smiled at Brandi "How you doin?" he asked shaking her hand.

When we were kids, Rafiq was a ladies' man very early in his life. As his female 'bestie', I definitely learned a lot of game from him and accepted all of his gifts along the way. I just never took him serious before that time I saw Rafiq at the prison while I was visiting my ex.

Now, the story was Fiki was out of the country, but I guess, his family didn't want it known that he didn't beat that gun charge after all.

Once Rafiq saw me, he always found a way to be on the detail to somehow see me every visit. We rekindled our cordial friendship and kept in touch until he started coming into visits with some girl named Karen. He claimed he was using her to get in to see me.

One day leaving the visit, Rafiq leaned over and told me, *that* would be my *last* visit to that prison to see my ex. I laughed at him, but he never cracked a smile. As we were standing in the space waiting to be let go from the visit, Rafiq kissed me before he walked off.

My stomach dropped. I felt high when I finally opened my eyes. He leaned down and whispered in my ear. "I'll be back for you" he bit my neck and walked away.

I remember standing there watching him walk out the room feeling super turned on, totally ignoring his warning. My slow self was looking forward to a visit in two weeks, that never came. Rafiq wasn't lying, that last visit was my *last* visit.

Corey, my now ex, had called and told me he put his son's mother back on the list. He claimed he needed to be there for his son because a *boy needs his father...Ok, first of all that wasn't even his son, well not biologically anyway.*

I didn't even fight it, I gladly let *her* take over that headache. So, when the money ran out on the phone, I never replenished it. *I BLOCKED HIM!! He couldn't even call me collect.* I was done with Corey.

But back to my night in town and Rafiq having me hemmed up against this truck. I mean he's not touching me but he's close as hell and I could barely move.

Rafiq shook Brandi's hand as he focused back on me. I noticed a few girls' attitudes on the sidelines. "I don't think your fans appreciate you being all up on me" I said as Rafiq backed me up more against his truck.

He put his arm up to block me from moving to the side as he stooped down and kissed my neck again. "I already told you before, you're *my* baby so I'll kiss on you every time I see you. I really don't care" he kissed my cheek and flagged his hand at the girls behind him.

I put my hand on his chest to back him up off me. "Yeah, that might have been cute had it not been almost three years since I last saw or heard from you" I said pushing him back an arm's length away.

Rafiq backed up, "My bad, what you got a dude now?" he asked smirking.

I paused and he moved in closer and right before I could answer, Rafiq grabs me around my wait and pulled me in closer and chuckled, "Like I thought, and even if you did have a dude, fuck him" he kissed my lips again.

I had no idea who *this* Rafiq was, but I was slightly intrigued with him.

Brandi cleared her throat, "No, don't mind me, so um yeah about my situation..." Brandi said waving her hand.

"My bad, you're waiting on me" I tried to walk away. "Here I come" I said looking back at Fiki.

He quickly offered to bring me home, I waved my hand at Brandi, "I uh...see so" I fumbled over my thoughts trying to think of a good reason as to why I couldn't go with him.

I hesitated and looked at my cousin hoping she'd save me, but she didn't. Once he offered a way for her to get the after-party faster, she was with it.

Brandi smiled. "No this is perfect because I'm going to his house" she handed me a key. "You're obviously in great hands, so now you don't have to rush *or feel like a third wheel*" she whispered then smiled at Rafiq. "Very nice to meet you" she shook his hand again and walked away.

Rafiq said he had to tell his crew he wasn't going to eat. I looked at him like he was crazy, "I didn't think you'd want to hang at the Waffle Hut" he said laughing.

"Why wouldn't I want to go get pancakes" I put my hand on my chest. "Fiki stop playing like you don't know I will fuck some pancakes up" I grew giddy at the thought of some fluffy flapjacks this time of morning.

He nodded his head laughing, "Yeah you will" he glanced over at me. "How long 'you here for?" he asked.

I stepped up inside his truck. "Until Tuesday" I replied

Rafiq closed the door and walked around the truck and climbed inside, "There's no way you're *not* staying with me" Rafiq laughed as he picked up his phone.

"Wait until I tell my momma you're out here" he played with the buttons on his dash.

I clapped my hands excitedly. "Awww, your mom, I love her. How is she?" I smiled in anticipation of his response.

He smiled showing off his chipped tooth. "She's good, I'll take you to see her tomorrow."

I clicked my seatbelt. "So, since I'm staying with you, can I *at least* go get my bag, so I can get out these shoes?" I inquired.

Rafiq turned on his navigation. "Put the address in" he said pointing to the screen.

I punched in Brandi's address then sent her a text knowing I probably wouldn't see my cousin again until we start preparing for her housewarming.

I looked over at Rafiq and thought about his kisses. I'll just say I'm seriously considering breaking my "no commitment/no kiss" rule just to see how good it really is with him *now*. Because if it gets better than that neck kiss...Chile, I'm in trouble.

"I *have* to be back on Saturday afternoon to help her cook and prepare for the party on Sunday" he nodded his head, smiling playfully.

"I'm serious Fiki" I said in a stern tone.

Rafiq rolled his eyes as he pulled out of the driveway.

"Noted, gotta be back by Monday" he winked his eye and laughed.

As we were leaving Brandi's house Rafiq decided against my objection to call his mother.

He is still such a Momma's Boy.

Chapter 5: Rafiq

'Yea, I got a lot goin' on...'

I moved South almost two years ago, of course my mom came shortly after.

"Ma, guess who's here" I blurted out as soon as she answered.

"Who Moop" she replied but I shushed her.

"Word Ma, obviously I'm in mixed company, why would you call me that?" I asked.

My mom went off. "Listen here, it's three in the goddam morning *Moopski*! You called my goddamn phone, now, what the hell do you want?" she snapped.

I quickly realized my mother didn't sound sleep. "Wait, why you don't sound like you're in bed" I questioned her upbeat tone.

My mom grew more annoyed with my line of questions.

"Mutha-, I'm 'bout to hang up..." she yelled into the phone. I took it off speaker as Jhonnie laughed.

"Oh, you're really stepping off the porch now ain't ya" my mother chuckled at me.

I put the phone back on speaker. "Say hi" I put the phone in front of Jhonnie.

"Hey Ms Shug" Jhonnie said

I could hear her smiling through the phone.

"Ooo this gotta be somebody from my hood because nobody calls me Ms Shug but folks back home" she said growing with excitement.

I looked at Jhonnie, "Oh my god Mom, just guess" I yelled into the phone.

"You don't have to guess Ms Shug, Hiiiii, it's Jhon-nie" she sang.

My mother gasped and yelled, "Oh my goodness MaJhonnie, I just asked Moop about you" she started speaking in falsetto tones.

I hurried up and ended the call. "Mom, I'll talk to you tomorrow or later on today. And don't think I forgot. You got some explaining to do! Alright Yolanda, later" I ended the call.

"You and your mom are so cute" she smiled as she applied some stuff to her lips.

"Can I tell you I'm really digging this whole look you got going on" I complimented her.

Jhonnie smiled as she looked in the mirror. "Aww Fiki, thank you and look" she held her foot up. "You remember these?" she asked holding her leg.

I had bought her two pairs of shoes, a bag and perfume back from my trip to Italy a few years back. "My mom picked those out, she said 'Get her these girls love peek toes" I said, and she laughed.

"It's *peep toe, not peek"* she corrected me.

We pulled into the parking lot, Jhonnie asked if we could by-pass going in. She'd rather take it back to my spot to chill, she explained her long day. I completely understood, so I told her I would get a menu. Jhonnie didn't need it, she told me her order.

"No need, pancakes with scrambled eggs with extra cheese and bacon" she said looking at her phone.

As I was walking to the door. I saw Iban standing by his car. I walked over to Iban's car, "Change of plans, my guy" I extended my hand.

Iban grabbed my hand and quickly bent down to try and get a good look at Jhonnie sitting in the truck.

"I see" he said jokingly.

I smiled and didn't realize I hadn't stopped smiling, until Iban's eyes grew wide as he joked about me being so geeked.

"I gotta meet this girl, yo ass ain't stopped smiling. He's like a little teapot, just bubbling over with excitement" he laughed with our other boy Frankie.

"Look *at* you, who is it? " Frankie joined in the joke.

"My *baby*..." I raised my eyebrows and nodded.

"*Get the fuck outta here, say word*" he said looking again.

I pushed Iban away as Vanessa aka Ness walked over. Ness is Iban's aunt, but he's older than her by a few months. We all grew up together, I think I was nine, maybe ten when I started hanging with them, then Frankie came to the block when I was twelve and it's been the four of us ever since.

I hurried up and ordered our food then told the guys, "Catch y'all later" I yelled making a beeline to my ride.

I drove through the city towards my house.

I couldn't believe Jhonnie just happened to be in town, thank God my original plans fell through, or I would have missed her. I carried Jhonnie's bag up the stairs into the front door.

Jhonnie walked inside and looked around the living room before turning to look at me, "You smoke?" she asked.

I glanced at her smelling the faint residue from this morning. "Yeah *Ma*" I replied at her shaking her head.

Jhonnie wasted no time getting comfortable. It was like 'old times, Jhonnie sat on my bed with her head scarf on, telling me about her latest drama at work and back home.

"Oh, my goodness Fiki does your mom or godmom age" she pointed at a picture of me standing with them from last Christmas.

I chuckled, "Her and my mom swear they young girls" I joked.

Jhonnie laughed, "I remember that summertime when I worked at one of her offices. I remember she was never there, but I worked hard, and I had so much fun! People kept saying we favored, but I didn't see it, I still don't see it" she stated putting the picture down.

Godmom had hooked Jhonnie up with a job during the summer before her junior year in high school. She said to put some money in her pocket.

The crazy part was I did not use to see their resemblance before, but with her hair cut short, I definitely see it, now.

Jhonnie pulled her bag over and laid it flat. "I'm going to take a shower and I'll see you in a minute" she said as she looked up at me.

I nodded my head and walked out of the room. I walked into my room while taking my stuff off. I walked into the bathroom and turned on the shower. I started emptying my pockets, I put my phone on the charger and walked back into the bathroom.

I was standing under the water, letting it beat against my face when I heard a knock on my bathroom door.

"Come in" I peeked out the curtain to see Jhonnie in her robe.

"Someone is at your door" she said.

I looked at her. "*My door?*" I repeated.

She nodded her head then I heard the knock get louder. I turned off the water and grabbed my towel. I ran down the stairs to look out the window.

What the fuck is she doing here?!

I turned to run up the stairs and Jhonnie shot me a look as she walked back across the hall into her room. "Maybe, I *should* stay at my cousin's house" she said as I walked by her and into the bedroom.

"Shut up" I playfully tossed my towel at her as I walked back down the stairs. I opened the door and stepped outside.

"Oh, I can't come in?" Tiffany asked as I closed the door.

"Hell naw, I thought you wanted to fix things with your son's father" I fired off throwing her words back at her.

Tiffany sucked her teeth and started to object.

"Listen, don't come by my spot unannounced, you lost that 'pop up' privilege" I said firmly.

Tiffany's mouth dropped. I opened the door and stepped back inside. "Night Tiff" I locked the door and cut the porch light out.

That was crazy! What the fuck was Tiff thinking?

I locked the door and turned to look right at Jhonnie sitting on the stairs, "Girls still love Fiki I see" she said as she got up and walked back upstairs.

I flagged my hand, "That was purely for your benefit it's been over a month since I talked to Tiff, she musta have seen me leave with you" I shared.

Jhonnie shook her head. "Listen, I don't want to cause you any issues" she said lightly.

I walked into my room and Jhonnie followed me. "We're just friends" she said.

She kicked off her shoes and removed her robe before climbing into my bed.

I stood with my hands around my waistband. "Whatchu doing" I walked over to the window and closed the curtains.

"Fiki, we used to always sleep in the same bed" she snuggled down into sheets.

"Yeah, we were virgins! A lot has changed since then" I sat on the end of the bed.

Shit! I sleep naked!!

I slid off my ball shorts and climbed in bed. Jhonnie waited until I got comfortable before she laid on my arm.

"So, let's start this over. Do you have a girlfriend Rafiq?" she asked.

I looked at her, "No, I don't have a 'girlfriend."

Jhonnie smirked and tucked her scarf. "Well, I don't have a boyfriend just in case you cared" she said.

I shook my head. "Not at all" but Jhonnie twisted her lips at me, knowing I was lying.

I just smiled and pulled her closer. "That's that man's problem, if you do."

I kissed her forehead and closed my eyes before long we both fell asleep.

The next day or rather when the sun came up. We were both scared out of our sleep by my phone ringing.

"It's my mom" I slid the phone off the dresser to answer the videocall.

"Hey Fiki" my Godmom said looking into the camera.

Jhonnie hurried up and ducked under the blanket.
"I heard you had company" she said smiling.

"Yes, your girl is here" I replied.

She smiled widely. "Awww, that's so nice, I want to take y'all to lunch! I know your mom can't wait to see her, right Shug" she yelled.

On cue my mother chimed in. "Can't wait to see my baby" she waved.

My godmom said she would text me the information. Then ended the call. The whole vibe was weird, but I pushed it aside as I read the thread of messages that came through my phone.

Jhonnie came from under the blanket. My phone chimed again, and I smiled, "You like seafood?" I asked.

Jhonnie nodded her head as she sat up in bed.

"I didn't think your Mom *or* your Godmom liked me all like *that*" she said.

I shrugged trying to think back to when everything changed with Godmom and Jhonnie. Usually, they *didn't* care for *any* girl I liked or even showed interest in, they'd always find *something wrong with her*.

Jhonnie got out of bed and walked into the bathroom. "Right? And it's like all of a sudden" she said.

I thought for a minute, but then blew it off.

"Well, let's see how this goes" I finished getting ready.

Jhonnie came downstairs looking like the 'young girl' I remembered. She had a scarf tied like a bow around her head and she did something with her hair, so it was curly in some places with bigger curls than in others.

Jhonnie had on her infamous white V-neck t-shirt with some wide leg gray pants and a denim jacket and some Chucks. It was simple but she looked sexy as hell to me. Jhonnie picked up her waist bag and put her hands behind her back to snap it in place.

"Ready?" she asked.

Jhonnie put on these big glasses and fixed her earrings.

"You're so beautiful" I grabbed and kissed her hand.

She smiled as she touched my face. "Aww thank you Fiki!"

We stepped out the door and she headed towards the truck. I walked over and opened her door. I recognized her slowing down her walk as she approached the passenger-side door.

She's testing me...

I remember growing up she would have to constantly explain to me that a man is supposed to open the woman's doors. Her smiling let me know, I passed.

We arrived at the restaurant and I pulled into valet, then walked in and gave the host my Mom's name. He led us to a secluded back area. You could hear my mom and Godmom laughing loudly as we approached the area. They both shrieked and jumped up as we came closer.

"Oh, my goodness, Ms. Dottie" she yelled.

Godmom hugged her tightly as my mom excitedly awaited her turn. I observed the whole thing in awe. After their little reunion, we all sat down and my Godmom started in with a million questions.

First one was, "Why'd you change your number?" my mother asked.

Jhonnie looked between us. It's been almost three years since I saw Jhonnie but, it's been since her sophomore year in college since *they've* last seen Jhonnie.

"It was nothing personal towards y'all, I had to disconnect from some people. I lost phones and a lot of contacts but when I heard about Uncle Shizz, I reached out. But whatever, I'm back now" she smiled as she shrugged her shoulders.

My Godmom leaned in, "How's that lady" she screwed her face.

Jhonnie shook her head. "Please don't bring her up. We're not speaking, she doesn't even know I'm here" she shared.

I looked at Jhonnie. "Your Godmom ain't too fond of *my* mother" she explained.

Godmom made a vomit gesture and sipped her water.

I looked at my mother, but she avoided my eyes. She smiled then told on herself. Whenever my mom is lying or hiding something, she'll keep tucking her hair behind her ears.

The waiter just walked over for our drink order, so I decided to let it go *for now!*

After lunch, Jhonnie asked if I could take her back to her cousin' house. I dropped Jhonnie off and headed straight to my mom's. When I rounded the bend towards my mom's house, I saw Godmom had a new car. I parked behind it. I walked inside to hear my mom and Godmom in the kitchen still laughing.

"Oh, hi Fiki" they both said as I walked in.

"When did you get here?" I sat down at the counter looking at my mom cleaning greens.

"Last night, why" Godmom took off her glasses.

I looked at my mom. "Is that why you were up this morning when I called you?" I asked.

My mom looked up. "No, I was with my man" she said with a serious face.

I cut my eyes at my mom. Not at all amused by her jokes.

"How long are you here for?" I asked.

I turned my attention back to my Godmom. She explained being in town looking at another property and handling other business.

We continued having small talk, but after her third time asking about *Ms Dottie,* and my mom tucking her hair each time, I called it out.

"Ok what's going on with y'all" my mom looked at Godmom and then she looked at us.

Godmom pushed her book away, "Ok so I was contacted by an old friend, through a new friend" she paused and wrung her fingers together. "I *think* Ms Dottie is my daughter." She blurted out.

I looked at my Godmom then shook my head. "*What do you mean you think she might be your daughter?*" I asked with the most screwed up face.

"You said that your daughter died" I reached for the refrigerator door.

Godmom nodded her head. "I thought so too, but after that summer, it was just a suspicion, but when I *saw her*, I knew she was my daughter. Then I saw this picture in some stuff that was in a bag I got after my husband died*"* she laid a picture on the table.

"Get the fuck outta here" I scoffed.

I put the soda back and walked over to my mother's liquor cabinet and grabbed her brandy.

"Bring out the tequila" Godmom yelled from the kitchen.

We sat at my mom's kitchen table and they relived the story of Godmom's tragic beginnings. It was a lot, more than I was prepared to hear.

I threw a shot back as I looked over at my mother. "I don't understand! I mean, I get it you were running to protect yourself and the baby but" I started to say.

Godmom cut me off. "Saying it today, knowing how it all played out is very different from being *in it* back then" she rebutted.

She explained how Joshua, her now deceased husband had people *everywhere* which was why she was hiding in Phillsboro; a town over three hours away.

"And he still found me but by then I was no longer a threat, his embarrassment was gone. By that time, he needed me" Godmom said looking at my mother.

My mom tucked her hair, I notice the crease in my Godmom's forehead like she *too* was hip to my mom's tell.

"I told Fiki, she reminded me of you" my mother said cutting into the silence.

I nodded my head. "Yeah, she did" I looked at my phone. "Jhonnie's ready, Ima catch y'all tomorrow" I kissed them both and walked to the door.

"Oh yeah, and Godmom tell my mom I'll box her dude head off, *her man*. Ey, tell her stop playing with me" I smiled before closing the door.

I thought over Godmom's story as I drove to pick up Jhonnie.

What are the odds that I befriend a girl as a kid who visited in the summer, only for us to grow up together and learn that she could possibly be the daughter of my godmother, the child she thought she lost at birth?

I had to get myself together, I pulled up to the house and Jhonnie came outside. I got out to open the door when I heard someone yell my name, "Hey Ski..."

I looked over to see Denisha walking up towards the house next door. I waved my hand as I opened the door for Jhonnie.

Jhonnie climbed into the truck after handing me a box. "A little sample of some desserts we're having tomorrow" she said with a smile.

I walked around the truck and climbed inside. "How you know her" she pointed at a girl standing in the driveway talking to the neighbor.

"Who *Denisha,* yeah she's from around my way" I answered.

Jhonnie looked at me. "Never, her name used to be Dennis" I shared accidentally.

Jhonnie turned to look again. "Shut up, that's a man" she exclaimed as she adjusted her mirrors to get a better view of Denisha.

I turned the car around and headed down the street out of the development.

"Wait until I tell Brandi, the 'sexy surgeon is on the DL" Jhonnie was typing a message on her phone.

"Don't do that" I said empathizing to Jhonnie that I shared something confidential with her. "I always tell folks if I didn't know Denisha from before I would have never known, you can't tell" I said.

That night, we stayed up all night talking, fell asleep laying across my bed with my head in her lap.

We woke up the next day, I took her to the water, let her clear her head. I stopped by my mom's house real quick, you know Jhonnie opted to stay in the car.

"So, when you coming back?' I asked as I backed my truck into my driveway.

"You got company" Jhonnie said looking into the side mirror.

I turned to see Morgan walking down the stairs of my house. Morgan was a cool girl I kick it with from time to time.

"This is nutty" I said as I got out of the truck.

Morgan walked over and immediately began apologizing.

"I know, you said never to just stop by without calling, but I lost my phone and I missed you and I was hoping" she said.

I cut her off. "Morgan, you're tripping" I said with my hands up.

She grabbed at my manhood. "You don't miss me; it's been too long for that" I stated.

Jhonnie walked by heading towards the door. "Can I get in I have to use the bathroom" she smiled and greeted Morgan as she walked by.

I walked over towards the door and unlocked it for her. I made sure Jhonnie got into the house, then carried her bags inside.

"Rafiq, are you kidding me" Morgan started her dramatics as I came back to the truck for some more things.

"Aye Morgan, what did you say the last time we were together" she reached for me, but I moved away from her. "No, what did you say" I repeated my question.

She thought for a minute then stomped her foot. "Come on Rafiq damn" she groaned.

I shook my head, "Naw, you gotta sit in that" I said.

"Okay I'll go for now but call me when your company goes home" she tried to kiss me, but I backed up.

I walked into the house to see Jhonnie looking in the refrigerator, seeming completely unbothered by Morgan's visit.

"You really need to go to the market" she said.

I held up a bag. "I did, got me some stuff for the week" I opened the bag of food and goodies my mom packed for me.

"Your mom is the best" Jhonnie grew more and more excited as each container came out of the bag.

"So are you *sure* you don't have a girlfriend" she asked biting into a donut. "Oh, this is so good" she said chewing.

I nodded my head as I put juice into the fridge.

"Morgan is a girl that I was dating but she quit me because I wouldn't go down on her" I said and immediately turned to explain.

I could feel Jhonnie stop breathing. She looked at me as she slowly bit into the donut.

"I don't have a problem going there, I'm just real cautious" I smiled at her starting to breath again.

"What about the girl from the other night" she asked. I looked at her, she was ready for a conversation.

I shook my head, "Nothing" she smirked, and I walked over towards her.

Jhonnie backed up against the counter. "Don't walk up on me" I cornered her and leaned down and kissed her neck.

"I'm waiting on you" I said between kisses.

She leaned her head back moaned softly in my ear, that shit turned me on.

"Mmm Fiki" she moaned as wrapped her arms around my neck.

I lifted her up and put her on the counter. I kissed down her neck and sucked the top of her breasts. I grabbed her legs and wrapped them around me.

She tightened her thighs around waist. "Can I have you?" I asked as I kissed her forehead then her lips.

Jhonnie looked at me and nodded her head. I was unfastening her boot when I stood up and our eyes locked, Jhonnie pulled me by my shirt and kissed my lips. I lifted her off the counter and carried her up to the room.

Jhonnie was kissing me, which was big, she only *'kisses guys she's serious with'* according to her. "I thought you only kiss your boyfriend?" I asked.

She smiled as she moved back onto the bed. "Well, I guess that makes you my boyfriend, *for now*" she smirked.

I stopped and looked at her. "Oh, for *now?*" I asked.

She nodded her head, "Rafiq, let's be for real. You've had two different women, knock on your door in less than two days. I'm no fool, I just wanted to kiss you" she shrugged her shoulder.

I looked at her. "Ima take a shower" I walked into the bathroom and cut the water on. I stood at the door, "You comin'?" I raised my eyebrow at her.

Jhonnie got off the bed. She unfastened her pants and walked into the bathroom.

"Don't play with me Rafiq, you're not really ready for me! But I'll play your game" she said sarcastically.

I closed the door behind her. "I'm not playing no game. I'll dead everybody for you. I'm your boyfriend, right?"

Jhonnie stepped into the shower. "Yup, for now"

I was on my knees in the shower drinking a mixture of water and Jhonnie when she jumped and not in a good way.

"You hear that" she grabbed the shower bar. "Somebody's at your door" she opened the curtain.

"*Fuck*" I grunted as I stepped out of the shower.

I wrapped a towel around me and put my feet in my Nike slides. "Who the fuck is this" I hurried downstairs. I walked to the door and opened it. "Karen, what are you doing here" I put my foot to block the door from her just walking in.

"Daddyyyy" my daughter screamed. I leaned out the door to meet her for a kiss.

"What are you doing, let us in" Karen pushed against the door.

I pleaded with Karen as she pushed even harder against the door.

"Please, give me an hour, I gotta tie up some loose ends and I'll come by the house" I quickly offered.

I don't think I ever prayed so hard in my *entire* life.

"One-hour *Rafiq*, and I'm not playing" Karen said as she rolled her eyes and walked back to her car.

Thank God my babymom decided not to show her ass.

I locked the door and ran back upstairs. Jhonnie turned the water off and came out of the bathroom holding her towel.

"So, I'm going to get dressed and you don't have to take me back to my cousins" she walked past me with her clothes in her hand. "I'm calling her now, to come and get me" she said pressing numbers on her phone.

I followed her into the guestroom as she packed her bag. I tried to explain but she stopped me. "Fiki, it's cool, this is the first time seeing you on some spur of the moment shit and it's been what? Three years" she looked up at me.

"You have your thing setup and it's cool, really it is" she quickly got dressed around her towel.

I didn't fight it, I just walked back to the room to get dressed. As I was tying my sneakers, Jhonnie walked into the room, "Brandi is on her way, I'm going to wait downstairs" she said as she backed out of the room. I grabbed my wallet and phone then followed her.

Well, was Brandi outside just waiting for her to call?

I thought to myself as I looked out the window to see her parked out front. I called out to Jhonnie as she stood at the door.

"Wait" I walked close to her and she held her hand up.

"Please Rafiq, just let me leave while I'm still on chill, I'm tryna be respectful of your life, but three visitors in three days? I'm sorry but that's a *huge* red flag for me" she looked up at me as she opened the door.

"Still my peoples though, *love when I see you though*" she said giving me the peace sign with a smile behind her fingers as I tried to kiss her.

She walked out the door and I grabbed her suitcase, "Go head I'll carry your bag" I followed her to the car.

I put her bag in the back, then waved at her cousin.

I leaned in to kiss her cheek, "I'll call you" I said in a tone that was moreso telling her, not asking her.

Jhonnie tilted her head, "Ole girl might not like that particular scent, you might wanna go wash your beard again. Hurry up now, you only have an hour" she winked at me as she got into the car and they left.

I smelled my top lip, "Shit but I love it" I went back inside to wash my face.

Chapter 6: Rebecca

'I might have started some shit...'

I woke up early to head downtown to get these sneakers I wanted the last time me and my best friend Jhonnie was in the city for drinks with her co-workers.

Jhonnie is so talented, she does some of everything. She's like a 'one-stop shop' kinda person. She works for herself, but she also works in the fashion world and courthouse so, she knows a lot of people. If she doesn't have it then she knows someone who can get it.

She's a super cool people person and she's all about connecting folks. Now that I think of it, it's very odd that all of this was going on around her and she had no clue. Usually I'm the one getting "juice" from her. But here I am with some 'juice' of my own. It started out small but now I'm so deep into it, how do I share it with her and not risk our friendship.

Let me just put this out there, my best friend loves to fight! Okay? Her favorite line before she snaps is, "And I'll never be too old for this…"

I'm just stating facts, have I had to feel her wrath a few times? I mean…I be irking people when I be on my drunk shit. Now in my best friend's defense, Jhonnie's not a fighter for sport, she doesn't pick fights but once she goes…it's dangerous because she won't stop,

So, let's go back to when this shit first started, it was about a year ago, I was leaving the store with my bags when I ran into Logan aka Lo, then referred to as "Ghostbastard" and his two brothers Levi & LeRoy.

"Hey Rebecca" Logan greeted as he stepped out the store I was walking past.

"Uh hey Lo" I waved and slowed down my pace.

"What's up witchu?" he asked.

I gave him *the look*. Logan acted shock at my statement.

"Don't act like we cool; you ghosted my friend" I snapped at him.

Logan shook his head as he put his arm around my shoulders. "It's really not like that" he said smiling.

I took a deep breath as I searched my bag for my ringing cell phone. I silenced the call and turned my attention back to Logan. One of the guys cleared his throat. Logan caught on and introduced his brothers.

"My bad these my brothers Levi & Boy" they both greeted me then asked about my friends.

Well, the one brother they called Boy did, Levi just kept locking eyes with me and smiling. And I must say, it was a welcomed gesture.

'My God he was so sexy!' I'm 5'7 so I was super short compared to them. Levi has to be about 6'2. He had long eyelashes and a beautiful smile. His hair was cut low, but it was dark and a nice beard. He has a slim-muscular build like a ball player. I loved his energy; he wasn't a goofball like Logan, but he was comical. As we walked, I checked out his getup: a simple white tee, cargo pants and air max sneakers.

'They smell good as a pack, like their chemistry was so bomb' I thought as I inhaled their combined aromas.

I glanced over and Levi smiled at me. I raised my eyebrow and smiled back at him. I looked over at Logan after he called my name to get my attention. Logan repeated my invite to some party and said he hoped I could make it and to bring some friends.

"See, just when I almost started liking you again" I shook my finger at Logan.

"You know I only have like two friends and you ghosted my best one" I fired back.

Logan looked over at his brothers and shook his head then repeated, "It wasn't like that Bec seriously" he dropped his shoulders.

I nodded, "I'm sure it wasn't" and then gave Logan the hardest eye-roll ever.

I reached into my bag and grabbed my trans pass, "You on the bus?" LeRoy asked as he unlocked the doors to an Audi truck.

I looked at the truck, "Um Boy is it, don't try and play me" I laughed. "I hate parking down-town, so I caught the train" I replied.

Roy lightened up his tone, "Oh naw, I was just asking my bad" he apologized.

He must have heard the judgement in his initial tone.

Levi took my bag out of my hand, "Which way you headed" he asked.

I blushed then smiled at Logan. He put his hands up as he backed away and stood by the back-passenger door.

I took my bag from Levi, then stepped closer to the stairs to go down to the train, "I'm cool, but thanks anyway" I waved my hand.

Levi smiled then shrugged, "You got it" he stepped back.

I immediately kicked myself when I saw Levi disarm a Porsche truck and Logan opened the passenger door to climbed inside. I dare not let him see me sweat so I turned on my heels to walk away, "Nice seeing you Lo" I yelled as I jogged down the stairs.

I had just enough time to run and get something to eat, take a nap if I decide to *pop out tonight*.

Oh shoot, I gotta go over to Jhonnie's to let Brutus out. Brutus is her mini schnauzer that she thinks is everybody's child when she decides to travel. I can't lie, I don't mind dog or house sitting for Jhonnie. Her new place has EVERYTHING.

Jhonnie had to go see her uncle, so I had to find a partner for the weekend. I was def going to this party. I scrolled through my 'good girlfriend phonebook', I text our mutual friend Jasmine and of course she was down to ride. You gotta keep a girlfriend that stays ready!

"Bet" I said to myself as I put my phone back in my bag, I pulled my hat down lower.

'My dumb ass...'

I thought as I laid my head on the window and I watched the buildings go by, I coulda been in a Porsche truck. I found myself thinking about Levi a lot that day.

I had just walked into my apartment from my errands when my phone chimed again. It was my cousin Randie, "Yo Cous" I said as I put the phone on speaker.

"What it do shawty?" he yelled.

I walked into my room. I began making my bed as my cousin tells me some story about his friend named, Pudd that's asking for my number for some other dude.

"You eva hear of the Murphy Brothers, you know Lo, Boy and Pudd Murphy, " he asked.

I thought for a minute. I stopped what I was doing and ran over to my phone, "Wait, now say that again?" I asked leaning into the phone.

Randie laughed, "Yeah right lemme find out you on the Murphy hitlist" he joked.

I sucked my teeth, "Hitlist my ass" I said becoming instantly annoyed and turned off. "Don't give nobody my number Randie, I'm not playing" I yelled.

He told me to "Be easy" then abruptly ended our call.

I decided I wanted to hang out tonight, so I sent Jas another text, I waited a few minutes, but I didn't hear back yet. I decided to take it down, I needed a nap. *'Sis was tired!'*

I walked into my room and climbed into bed. "I'll call her when I get up". Even thought I had closed the curtains, I still put on my eye-mask. I wanted a good sleep.

My phone chiming scared me out my sleep. I felt around on my bed looking for phone. I lifted my mask and peeked at the screen.

"Dammit" I yelled dropping my mask back over my eyes.

I dropped the phone after being blinded by the light in the dark room. After turning down my screen, I was able to focus on a message from Randie. I climbed out of bed and walked into my bathroom.

I was putting my hair in a bun when I received a picture from him.

I gasped, "Oh my god…" I fawned over the photo he sent me.

I must have taken too long to respond because he sent another one. It was pictures of the dude asking about me. It was Levi and dammit he looks good.

"Ok Randie on the lookout" I said out loud.

I smiled as I stared hard at Levi's sexy ass!!! He's more like six feet tall standing next to him, because Randie said he was 6'2.

Levi's muscular with a perfect smile like he had braces as a kid. He has a dark haircut with a beard and the softest looking lips. He looks mixed and I bet his dad is black. His swag is too dope to have a white pop, is that terrible to say?

He even looks like he smells delicious. He had on a black V-neck shirt looking simple and sexy with these dog tags around his neck.

"Come out to Sharkiees bar over off 58th and Franklin" Randie had sent another text.

I scrolled thru my phone for Iynesha number. Iynesha, or Neesh lived in that part of the city and she was always ready.

Jas said she was down for whatever, so I text her, "Goin to Sharkies you rollin" within two minutes Jas and Neesh responded they was with it. Now I had never been to Sharkies but here goes nothing.

'What am I going to wear?'

I packed a bag to take with me because I had to go to Jhonnie house to let out her dog. She won't be back in town until Tuesday. I threw the bag in my trunk and pulled out the garage heading to Jhonnie's then out the Eastside to Sharkies.

I got there faster than expected, so I decided to tie together any loose ends as I waited. I flipped down my visor and looked in the mirror. My lashes were still popping. I added some gloss and smoothed the sides of my bun. I looked at myself one more time before getting out.

"Alright, Bitch let's do it" I said giving myself a good pep talk. I opened the door just as Neesh pulled up with her music blasting.

"I swear you skinny bitches irk me" Neesh said as her big booty slid out her truck.

Neesh was a plus sized girl but she carried it so cute to me. She was more solid than fat, if my vote mattered. Plus, her ass was most of it. I wanted one but momma ain't give me nothing but some long hair, nice boobs and flawless skin.

"You look cute Neesh" I said opening my arms to embrace her hug. "Making me feel overdressed but who cares right you're here" I smiled hugging her again.

Neesh looked at me, "And as usual you're so extra! Girl, Sharkies is an after-hours, local dope boy hood bar. This ain't the Jhonnie bougie bar type scene, you're used too" she declared.

I looked down at my dress and heels then over to Neesh leggings, with an off the shoulder type shirt and some Gucci slides. "Are you serious?" I asked feeling a little disappointed but yet, intrigued.

Neesh went to answer but Jasmine blew her horn scaring the shit out of both of us.

"Oh, that's right! Jhonnie did go visit Uncle Sammy" Neesh said laughing.

She was referencing a joke she made some time back that I only hang out with Jas whenever Jhonnie ain't around. I mean it's true but I'm not being sneaky. It's only because Jhonnie and Jas aren't getting along right now.

"What sometimes all friends of friends ain't friends" I said shifting my weight. "And yes, I love Jhonnie more soooo" I twisted side to side. "I mean…she's my best friend, but Jas is cool. I like hanging with her" I said fidgeting.

I threw my hand in the air and smacked my side feeling judged. I couldn't let it stop there even though Neesh didn't say a word.

I continued justifying. "Shut up! Ok, so what Jasmine's my side piece. She's cool with it…I think" I cut my eyes over at Neesh.

I turned to look over at Neesh and she laughed.

You are *so fuckin* extra" she laughed as she popped gum in her mouth.

Jasmine got out of her car with a low-cut shirt, capris and some cute wedge sandals with a messenger bag, "I knew this bitch would do too much" Jas joked as she zipped her bag, then reached for a hug.

"Listen, in my defense I'm prowling so 'keep in mind that I'm an artist' I'm serious AND sensitive about my shit..." I said quoting one of my favorite artists, as I did the "viola" motion up and down my black fitted dress.

I kicked my foot behind me to show off my black strappy sandals.

"I see you" Jasmine said as she hugged Neesh. "Hey Sis" she smiled.

Jas popped her lips as she put on her lip gloss and gave Neesh a look.

Neesh nodded her head. "Right but we're going into a bar, in *the* hood, and a bunch of fucking dope boys. You're 'bout to walk into a den little lamb but do not say you weren't warned. Come on let's go so you can get your prowl on" Neesh said as she turned me by my elbow.

I turned around and did an old skool dance then we all laughed. "Did she just bust out with the Wop?" Jas asked in a concerned tone.

I started feeling myself, as I walked between 'my two underdressed escorts'. Jasmine gave me the finger and Neesh told me not to 'play with her' but I did...

I put on my stuffy stuck-up accent, "Iynesha, please be a love and slow down, slow down I say. I can only move but so fast in these heels in this dreadful parking lot" I faked complained.

I turned to joke with the couple walking by, "Things you do when your security team wants chicken wings" and gave a stuffy laugh.

"She gets on my nerves" Jas said from behind me.

"What I joke...I kid" I said as I hugged Neesh from behind.

I had ran into her because she stopped so suddenly. She had 'that look' on her face as she turned with her hands on her hip, "What I say" I hugged her again,

"Awwe Neesh I'm sorry, don't be like that!" I turned her around, "Come on let me buy you a drink" I shared.

Jasmine shook her head, "We might as well be her security, the way we always keeping somebody off your pretty ass" she said laughing.

Neesh laughed "Okayyy" as she held her hand up for a high five.

I slapped both their hands down, "Uhn uh don't do that! Y'all make it seem like I can't handle myself" I flagged them off.

Okay moment of honesty, I have been known to need assistance a time or two, but it was never my fault. Last time we went out "they" started with me. And my dumb ass not even realizing it was a lot of *them* and wouldn't shut up. Thank God for Jas because she stood tall with me. I love her for always having my back.

We walked in Sharkies and I immediately wanted to go back outside. Now don't get me wrong it was a nice spot, but I walked in and looked right into Levi's eyes. He smiled at me as he was talking to his friend. I felt like my name coulda been Lambert, these guys were very aggressive, but I wanted Levi.

Oh my god, 'is it bad I want to give it to him already? Like I want to put it in a cute box and carry it over to him and say, "Hold out your hands' and gently lay it on him'.

It was very trying but I kept it cute and walked behind Neesh to the bar across the room. Three dudes got up and let us have their seats at the bar. I sent them a round for their generosity.

The vibe was cool, and I kept finding myself meeting eyes with Levi. It didn't take long for us to start flirting with each other as he watched me from different corners of the room. I was giving him the eyes, you hear me.

We flirted thru the mirror, from across the room, I even watched as he bopped to his song on some chill shit. Surprised myself when I didn't start cheesing at the bar when I looked up in the mirror to see him walking over towards me. I played it cool and sipped my drink.

Levi came behind me and put his hands on each side of me, on the bar. Then he leaned down real close. His beard tickled my neck as he got even closer and touched that spot just behind my ear with his lips as he whispered, "I came to say, you look beautiful tonight" he leaned in to say.

I closed my eyes as he told me he was glad I came out.

"Oh yea?!" I asked smiling.

I heard him whisper as I opened my eyes to see myself all leaned back on him moving to a beat. Not only did I get lost in the song, but it wasn't the song that was playing in the bar, so I'm all slow grinding on this man to *Shake it fast*. I covered my face, completely embarrassed.

"It's cool, I can dig it" he smiled as he turned to look around the room.

Oh my god!! He smelled delicious. I giggled but quickly composed myself. Levi leaned in again and whispered, "I'm tryna see you lata" he kissed my cheek.

He tapped on the counter and signaled for the bartender,

"Ayo Manny, for they tab" he pointed from Neesh to Jasmine, which included me in the middle, "Whatever they want" then pointed at himself.

Neesh yells. "Thanks Tuck, just so you know I'm gettin' food to go too" she gave him the thumbs up.

Levi nodded his head, "I already know" he gave her a side hug and shook Jasmine's hand, "Y'all enjoy! Let me know if you need anything else" he said as he leaned down and whispered. "Lata" in my ear.

He put his hand on the small of my back and pressed lightly into my side as he walked away. I just nodded as I fought back a smile.

I turned to give Neesh a look, "Bitch! Do you see him?" I asked.

Levi has no right smelling the way he's smelling. Oh my god! I want him. I turned to watch him talking to Logan. *Yeah, I want him!*

Neesh leans over, "Rebecca, you are not ready for good ole Mr. Tucker" she joked.

I looked at her, "Who the hell is Mr. Tucker?" I asked sipping my drink.

Neesh laughed "You gon soon find out" she laughed as she turned to talk to her brother Justin.

I ignored her comment as I watched Levi walk through the room. I noticed he was doing a lot of handshaking. I made a mental note to find out more about Levi aka Mr. Tucker and why was he was doing all this schmoozing.

It didn't take long before my ass started getting sleepy. I really thought I was cool. I remember walking outside as I was trying to find my keys.

I heard Jasmine yelling for me to stop, then Neesh grabbed me. I remember a bunch of ruckus, then some loud music, I got into a truck and that was it. Lights out!

I gasped to catch my breath as I jumped up and I opened my eyes finding it real hard to focus.

"Where the hell am I" I sat up looking around. The sun was up but the room was dark.

"You're home"

I peered into the corner. "Levi" I asked trying to see into the dark corner.

He moved up. "Yeah man" he replied in a low voice.

I sat completely up then I realized I was still dressed, and I began to panic. "Oh my God, why am I wet" I jumped out of the bed and looked around the room.

"Aww *shit*" I collapsed onto the comforter and immediately started taking the sheets off the bed.

"Yo, you good" he asked as he stood up.

I walked to the other side of the bed, "This is not my house, this is my best friend's house, that has OCD. She flips out when people wear their *outside* clothes and sit on her bed let alone be in it, like under the covers" I groaned again.

He nodded his understanding. "Oh, my bad" he sat back down.

"Wait, what are you doing here? How the hell did *we* end up here" I asked.

He started to explain but started to laugh. "*You* told me to bring you here. Then once we got here you got sick, so I ain't wanna leave you. You kept getting sick in your sleep" he shared.

I looked at him, "What do you mean 'I got sick?" I asked.

He sat back in the chair. "You got sick" he repeated in the same tone.

"You threw up in my truck, in the hallway and over there" he pointed. I jumped back and covered my mouth as I walked to where he was pointing.

"Oh my god, Jhonnie is gonna kill me" I felt my nerves building.

"I mean I cleaned it up as best as I could but since you over here tripping about your peoples, Ima call my crew to come clean her whole spot." Levi said as he stood up,

Levi pulled out his phone and I walked across the hall to the laundry room. "So how the heck did I wind up with you and where is my car?" I asked after looking outside and not seeing my car out front where I usually park.

Levi started laughing, "Whatchu mean, 'how'd you wind up with me' you got into my truck and told me to take you home" he replied.

I looked at him like he was crazy. "No, I didn't" I objected.

Levi pulled out his phone, "What's baby girl name again, you know the big jawn you were with, Jay sister" he asked.

I flipped the sheets open, "Iynesha" I yelled over the noise.

He nodded, "Yeah Neesha ask her she was there, matta fact, y'all was arguing when I pulled over by ya car" Levi was looking at his phone as he was speaking.

I started making up the bed, "Arguing? Me and Iynesha?" I asked.

Levi laughed, "Yeah man, call her. I wouldn't bullshit you" he stated.

I looked around the room. "Where is my phone?" I asked.

"Right there" Levi pointed to the nightstand.

I walked over and scrolled to Neesh name and pressed the call button. The phone rang twice before she answered, "Bitch, why are you calling me this early? Why aren't you sliding down on Tuck's meat stick?" she asked sounding like she was under her bed.

I couldn't get the phone off speaker fast enough. Levi's eyes got big, and he fell back in his seat laughing, "Ey ask her again, spit that hot shit to her Neesh" he yelled.

I threw the pillow at him then turned back to the phone call.

"What-ev-a, girl no I'm calling to find out what happened last night?" I lowered my tone.

Iynesha started laughing, "Here you go, as usual yo ass drank too much and got mad cause we wouldn't let you drive" Neesha said.

I looked over at Levi playing in his phone. "In true 'Rebecca fashion,' you made a scene trying to fight Jas, so I grabbed you. That's when the boys pulled over next to us. And then you told Tuck you were riding with him" she ended her story and Levi nodded his head.

"Shut up Neesh" I replied as Levi threw his hands up then nodded his head as she confirmed his story.

"That's what happened!" he exclaimed.

"What? You told him to take you home" she began telling another story.

I looked at a grinning Levi. H*e ain't gotta be that damn sexy!*

"You made Lo get out the car and you got in the passenger seat" Iyesha said.

"Ey Neesh tell her what else she did" Levi yelled and I covered my face.

Iynesha busted out laughing "Oh, after you kicked Lo out the front seat, I tried to get you out the truck, that's when you straddled Tuck and kissed him" she said flatly.

I know I was beet red; I couldn't even look up. I looked back at the phone, "And then what" I asked as Levi leaned over putting his phone in his pocket.

"Whatchu mean, Lo got in the car with Neesh like, 'I guess you taking me home" they both started laughing.

"We came here, and you started throwing up" Levi said applying chapstick to his lips.

Neesh yelled. "Ahh man, nooo you wasted it" she laughed and started coughing.

I ended the call. "Bye Iynesha"

I looked over at Levi completely embarrassed. He waved it off, "It's cool" he said.

I plugged my phone back into the charger. I stood with my back to Levi not knowing what to say. Thank God he broke the silence,

"Listen, do you need your car this morning? I got Lo and Pudd bringing it but not til after three" he advised.

I turned to see him walking towards the door. "You're leaving?" I asked trying not to sound too disappointed.

"Why you want me to stay?" he turned and smiled.

I tried not to smile at him. "I mean I'll understand if you have to leave, you probably gotta get home, can't be staying out all night" I said sarcastically.

Levi nodded as he fished around in his pocket looking for his keys.

"You're probably right I mean the sun is up" he walked out the room.

I heard him going down the stairs. I hurried up and walked out into the hallway to talk to him over the railing.

Levi looked back at me, "I'll catch you lata" but his tone was more of telling not asking.

'Lata' I giggled mimicking him as I shook my head, "We'll see" I yelled, and he smiled.

Levi opened the door and gave a head nod before he walked out and closed it behind him. I moved further down the hallway so I could see him walk to his truck. I watched him pull off. I watched until his lights disappeared from my sight. I know that was so corny.

It was still early; I decided to try and go back to sleep. I needed to clean up though. I was in the shower when someone knocked at the door. I managed to get out in time to catch them.

"Can I help you?" I asked staring at a cute young girl's back.

The girl turned around and greeted me, "Hi, Mr. Murphy sent us over for cleaning services.

I looked at her, "Oh my god, I thought he was playing" I opened the door to let her and another girl inside.

They brought in their equipment and got right to it. I loved everything about them, what I loved even more was they left smell goods for each room after they cleaned. They didn't have to clean much because Jhonnie cleaned before she left. Like I said, she has OCD, so she has a whole weekly routine.

Jhonnie called just as they were leaving, "Hey Tink how are you" we had small talk, but it was cut short because she had to go. She was going out to lunch with her uncle. I locked the doors, then set the alarm before running back upstairs to get back in the bed.

I had just laid on the bed when the doorbell chimed. After flipping around in bed throwing a tantrum, I made it back downstairs, "Who is it" I looked out the window, "Hey Lo" I said opening the door.

"Yo Champ, you good" Logan smirked as he walked inside dangling my keys in front of me.

"We took it to the car wash; you need to be 'shamed of that car" he said joking but I could tell he was serious.

I snatched my keys, "What-ev-a" I said pushing him.

Logan walked back to the door, "You coming out tonight right?"

I shrugged, "Who knows" I said not being sure about too many things right now.

Logan opened the door and looked back at me. "Ayo so where's Jhonnie?" he asked looking around.

I scoffed at him, "Outta town with her new man, why?" I snapped at him.

Logan blew raspberries, "Oh please! Speaking of a new man, so uh you're feeling my bro, sumthin' heavy I see" he said with a huge grin.

I fought hard but I couldn't help but to smile. Logan lifted his hat to scratch his head, "Uh huh look at you" he knocked on the door and walked outside.

I reset the alarm and this time went to Jhonnie's private space on the upper level and went to sleep.

Brrrrrr brrrrrrr my phone vibrating on the table woke me up. I click the message notification 'Damn how long did I sleep?'

"Where you at" I read through one eye before sitting up.

"I decided to stay in after all" I giggled as I typed back.

'Oooo is somebody looking for me…'

Chile, my poor stomach wouldn't behave. My head hurt a little and I kept breaking out into sweats. I felt terrible. I know I shouldn't drink the way I do, but you can't feel it when you're sitting down. That shit always hits me once I get outside! I gotta do better. When? I don't know so, please don't ask again.

"Not feeling good, still in bed" I put my phone down and walked down into the kitchen. My hair was in a messy bun. I had on a tank top and panties. I grabbed some ginger ale and crackers then headed back upstairs.

I looked in on Brutus, he was chilling in his room for the night. Yes, he had his own room. It was a closet, but it was big for a dog. He was sleeping on his bed. *Spoiled ass dog!*

I went back upstairs and climbed back in bed. I leaned over to check my phone to see a missed call. Levi? I pressed his name, and the phone rang.

"What's wrong" his voice was so masculine yet caring.

I smiled, "Awww look at you" I said feeling special.

He started talking to somebody in the background then came back to the phone. "I thought I was gonna see you tonight" he sounded very disappointed.

I did the *nasty girl* dance to music in my head but stopped as I started talking. "Sorry I just couldn't get it together" I replied.

Levi chuckled, "Yo ass *is in da cooker*" he said laughing.

Before I could respond Levi had to end the call. "Ima hit you right back" I dropped the phone on the bed and picked up the remote. I turned on Netflix.

A few minutes later, my phone chimed, "I wanna see you"

I smiled. "Well, come see me" I text back.

A few minutes later Levi called. "Let me handle this business with my brother right quick then Ima come wherever you are, cool?" he asked.

I agreed. "Don't go to sleep" he ended the call.

I text him letting him know I was still in Alto Hills. He replied back "Solid", and I threw a happy fit in the bed.

I jumped out of bed and danced into the bathroom, I had to shit, shower and stretch. Yes, it's a whole process. Thank God I got waxed last week. I was putting on my body butter when the doorbell chimed.

Either he's mad early or this ain't for me. I tied my nightgown and walked to the door. It was Levi. I opened the door, and he walked in slowly because the house was dark. I closed the door and took him downstairs to the sitting area.

This jawn nice", he said as he walked through the house.

After we sat on the loveseat, "It's over already?" I asked him about the party.

Levi moved a pillow out of his way, "Oh nah it's still rocking, but when you told me you wasn't coming I ain't wanna be there no more" he said.

I twisted my lips at him.

"No bullshit" he held his hands up.

I rolled my eyes and walked over to grab the remote. "You smell good" he said as he adjusted himself on the couch.

I played like I was not checking him out, I promised myself I was gonna do *this* different.

We started talking, shared a few laughs then next thing I know we both fell asleep. We were shaken awake by Brutus biting his laces.

"Damn what time is it" he stood up and quickly bent over trying to hide himself, "My bad where's your bathroom" he walked away looking embarrassed about his morning wood.

I wasn't! Sis was definitely here for it..."I'll be right back" I said as I went upstairs to freshen up.

When I came back downstairs Levi was sitting in the kitchen talking on his phone. I walked over to the sink to put on some hot water for my morning tea.

"I gotta meet up with my family for 'Dunch' later" Levi said as he put his phone in his pocket.

I looked at him. "You mean 'brunch" I said thinking he said it wrong.

He shook his head, "I don't know about the type dudes you're used too but I'm no dummy. I know how to say the word" he nicely told me, and I let it go.

"It's some shit my brother Pudd made up. It's breakfast, lunch and dinner on a Sunday. He named it that because we can't get up for breakfast, so we just meet like three-ish and rock out until we get tired" he explained.

I laughed. "That's cute" I replied.

Levi nodded as he stood up, "Whatchu got planned?" he asked.

I looked around, "Laundry...I always wash clothes here on Sundays but other than that I don't have any plans, especially since you sent ya cleaning crew through here" I thanked him for that.

He looked up from texting, "Ok so, can I see you after dunch?" he asked.

I decided to be playful. "Let me find out you like me" I giggled.

Levi shrugged, "Ok, I think I've already made that clear so can I see you or not" he repeated his request.

I was loving his forward attitude so far. I folded my arms across my chest, "I guess just call me when you're done" he tapped the counter as he walked over and kissed my forehead.

"Lata?" he asked walking away.

"Uhn huh, lata" I replied.

Levi nodded his head as he walked out the door.

Of course, he messaged me the entire time throughout "dunch", but I thought it was cute.

My phone chimed between our messaging; it was Jhonnie. "Hey Tink" I greeted my friend.

"Girl, this world is waaayyy to small. So, I'm down here with Unc and I learn my Aunt Nay moved a half hour from him, so I go for a visit. I'm cooling with my cousin and she's talking 'bout this guy she met with because her bisexual boo wants to have a threesome. Girl, she shows me a picture of the guy they decided on...why is it Rhyon???" she yelled.

I gasped, "Noooooo, not again" I started laughing.

"It's not funny! Why does it seem like my boy cousin's from one side always end up messing with a girl cousin from another side?" Jhonnie asked.

"Well, Jhonnie, you are related to some of everybody. You got like ten sides to your family" I joked but not at all exaggerating.

Jhonnie had her parent's sides then she is super tight with all their spouses and their families. And now with the rumor that her Dad *ain't* really her father, that means there's a whole 'notha side.

"So, I'm just calling to tell you that I'm going to Brandi's for a week, then I'll be home" she explained and then ended the call.

Now I have two more weeks to figure out how tell Jhonnie about Levi. I know she gon be pissed, I mean with him being *Ghostbastard's* brother and all.

Chapter 7: Leviathan

'Ima Murphy, I'm the chill one...'

"So Lee, what's the deal with you and Bec" Logan asked as he lit his blunt.

I flipped the sun visor back up, "Shorty bad right?" I asked thinking about that kiss she gave me that night at the bar.

"I definitely got my shovel out for the young misses...definitely diggin' her" I joked as I looked out the window.

Rebecca was the friend of Jhonnie, the girl Lo met at the airport.

Logan looked over at me, "I know! I see you been running behind her ever since she yoked yo ass up in the parking lot that night" he joked.

I let out a loud groan as I wiped my face. "Maann, you have no clue bro" I said.

Lo nodded his head, "Tuck, I was there I saw that shit! She slobbed you down like..." he hit my arm trying to find the words.

"Bruh she's been wanting to do that shit for quite some time, I'm here to tell you" he declared.

I laughed at Lo bringing up my old nickname. "You sure you ain't know her before now" he asked.

I shook my head, "You shot out for bringing that name back, I've been chilling" I smiled.

Leroy, 'Roy da Boy' or just Boy, my older brother started calling me "Tucker...tuck her" because he said I always kept a bad thing tucked away somewhere. And I usually did, but Rebecca seemed different. I could chill with her. But I couldn't let my brother know that we really just started kicking it, but I was *really* digging her.

I bit my bottom lip thinking about what Logan said about that night at the bar. It felt like some kinda message sending kiss.

"I'm glad she made the first move, so now I won't feel as bad when I finally trash her" I announced to my brother.

Logan tapped my arm to interrupt my thoughts. He blew some smoke out the cracked window before handing me the blunt.

"Listen, you heard what Pops said about Jhonnie, so just remember they're best friends which means she's going to be around, so you might want to play nice with Becs" he advised.

He turned the music down. "Plus, I like her, Rebecca is cool peoples for real" Logan said as he turned onto Boy's street.

I thought over Logan's suggestion, "I hear you. You're right, Ima chill" I said reclining my seat.

He looked in the backseat then told me to pull my seat up so Boy could have room.

Lo took the blunt out the ashtray, "Mmmm" Lo blew out a lil smoke, "Dawg, and not for nothing, you need to be more focused on figuring out whatchu gon do when Tina crazy ass find out" he laughed.

I shook my head, "Maan, Tina ain't gon do nothing" I flagged my hand.

Tina was my first everything in this dating world. She's the one that, 'no matter what I did, said or who I fuck with' she's gon always come when I call and even sometimes when I don't call.

Let's just say she's been there for at least fifteen years. But she recently moved in with her dude *after* putting our baby in a jar, so I'm not tryna hear her mouth about too many things I'm doing these days.

"Ion know Tuck, if Rebecca is anything like her homie, you ain't never had *her* before! *You* might not be ready. You know you only had like one real girlfriend in your whole life" Logan laughed and started coughing as he passed me the blunt.

I ignored him and changed the subject. "So anyway, before Boy get in the car" I checked to make sure he didn't come outside. "Why ya brother bring his sneak 'ya mean' over to my shit" I blew out the window.

Lo looked at me and howled laughing. "Wait, not ya spot off the highway? Noooo, not that night I saw you and Bec" he asked sounding in distress.

I cut my eyes at Logan. "Maaannnn, I had to get that shit out before Boy get in here. You know how that guy gets when you talk about Pudd and his *lifestyle*" Logan nodded his head in agreement.

"Naw, you mean Pop" Lo tapped my arm then corrected.

I acted like I had originally said it wrong. "That's right" I snapped my fingers pointing at Logan.

Boy intentionally stopped calling our brother his nickname, Puddin Pop. Our Mi-Mi named him, and we started just calling him Pudd. But once he came out as liking both men and women, Boy calls him Pop. Childish right? I know...

Logan and I laughed playing back Boy's reaction when Pudd finally confirmed for us that his 'block is a two-way street!'

The family was sharing their thoughts after Pudd *came out* to us when Boy just stood up and opened the door to leave. He turned to look at Pudd, "You're my brother, I'll always love you, but I don't want to hear about that shit, I don't want to see that shit and from this day forward ya *muthafuckin* name is Pop" he shrugged and stepped outside. "That's all I got" he said and then closed the door.

We knew Boy took it hard, those two were closer than the rest of us. We loved our brother so out of respect for our older brother, Logan and I keep our talks about Pudd between us.

Our brother, LeRoy da Boy can't stand that Pudd is bisexual. I personally feel like, *'Who that man do is none of my business just don't do it in my shit!'*

My dad has four sons and I love my brothers no matter what, bottom line, no questions asked.

So Pudd likes girl and boys. We all have shit with us, like my brother Boy, he can't stop having kids. He stays popping up with a new babymom. Logan, he's the most savage but he also can be the nicest one out of us all.

Of all my brothers, I'm the most chill. Total opposite of my baby brother, Logan but a calmer version of both he and Pudd. Pudd has always been the "hype" brother. He goes too far, legally or illegally; it didn't matter. Over the years, Pudd had no problem doing the time. He started out in juvie, county jail and progressed to state prison. He chilled out when there was talks of him being charged as a career criminal on his next offense.

He's another one that doesn't play any games about his brothers. He's forever down to go first and talk about that shit later. Even though Pudd can be reckless, he's still not as bad as Logan when he gets started. It's one of the reasons why if we bring Logan in on anything, we all must decide and agree on it first.

Yes, there is a criteria, for what we've come to call 'Bringing in The Baby'. It has got to be all facts because we know once he's in and shit gets heavy, he's not gon' back down.

Logan has always been an *off to the races* with *it* type of guy. There has been rumors in the streets, from what I hear our baby brother is a G. He's not in an official gang, but he does have a tight crew. They've been running together for a while now. Since like junior high school. Him and his one homie Bop being the tightest; they've been close since babies.

I turned the music down, "Ayo so whatever happened with Pops and Jhonnie's moms, did they ever clear that shit up" Logan shook his head and shrugged.

"You ain't never *nah mean* with her did you" I asked before he went into his story.

Lo took a deep breath as he cut me a look then blew out hard. "Naw but I wanted too, it just never went there, super glad about that" Lo answered his ringing phone. "Hold on...Yerp" he said into the receiver.

Just then my phone chimed. I looked at the message, "*Oh so since when do we let the new hoes drive Betty*" it read.

I backed right out of that message and put my phone in the cup holder. Tina musta seen Rebecca driving my car back to her side of town, that's a whole 'notha story

'Ion feel like Tina today'

I think I need to keep Tina on chill anyway. I ain't feeling her right now, her corny boyfriend called me like two weeks ago. She got some nerve asking me about anything I got going on, she better act like she knows, she broke the rules this time. *This* time the balls in *my* court. She made her choice when she went to that clinic. Now, I'm busy besides, I think I gotta new boo.

After handling some business with my brothers, I had them drop me off to Rebecca's.

"Ima drive *Betty* back home" I gave Logan and Boy dap as I walked away calling Rebecca's phone but got her voicemail. After calling her a few more times and sending a text message, I decided to wait for somebody to come out, but nobody ever came. I looked over her building directory.

I rang the buzzard, and she called my phone as she let me in. I stepped onto the elevator and pressed the button.

The doors opened, as soon as I stepped off the elevator, I saw a door to my left swing open.

"Over here" I heard Rebecca's voice. As I walked towards the door, I stutter stepped a little because I could smell her, and that shit smelled dangerous. I stopped at the door, "That's how you doin' it? See, now I'm tryna be a gentleman..." I announced walking inside.

She stepped from behind the door, and I dropped my head. She had on a long fitted shiny nightgown that showed the tips of her toes.

"I was getting ready to get in bed" she replied moving back.

I stepped inside and she closed the door. After hugging me she rambled off questions like my blood wasn't rushing to my midsection, I could barely think straight.

"How was your time with your brothers? Did you eat? Are you thirsty?" she asked.

I nodded my head as I followed her into the kitchen.

"It was cool, real productive. I'm not hungry but I'll take some juice" I said sitting at the counter.

She pulled out a pitcher of juice and poured me a glass. I took a sip of my drink as I watched her walk around the kitchen. I couldn't stop looking at her. We made small talk; it was mad comfortable. She talked to me about her day and asked questions about mine.

I looked up and she was looking at me, so I smiled at her. She threw the sponge on the sink as she sucked her teeth.

"Do you have a girlfriend" she turned on the water. "Or someone that thinks she's your girlfriend" her tone was very sharp.

I chuckled at how frustrated she had gotten, it happened real quick. I repeated the question in an effort to be playful.

"Do I have a *girl*? The way you describe it!? I would say, yeah, I got a girl! But not really, I mean she not only has a man, but she also lives with him so technically she's not my girl" she started to talk.

I held my finger up to stop her from interrupting my next point.

"So technically, I could say 'no' but that last part you threw in there, even though she lives with her guy, *she* definitely would still say *I'm her dude* if you asked her" I took another sip of the juice.

"She wouldn't happen to drive a blue Honda, would she?

"This juice good as hell" I tried to change the subject. I looked at the glass and asked for some more. As she poured my drink, I put some chapstick on my lips.

She turned around and slid the glass over. "Ooo ya lip gloss is poppin" she joked.

I scowled my face and shook my head, "Shut that down, Ion wear no damn lip gloss" I wiped my lips with a napkin.

She snapped her fingers in the air, "No, come on stay focused, so you're a *heartbroken side dude...of the girl that drives the blue Honda. Go head continue...*" she tapped her nails against the counter.

I was shocked at her bluntness, I must admit she made my eyes widened, "If that's what you call it, but I'm not a side dude, so I don't follow 'side dude' rules and I'm far from heartbroken" I replied, and she shook her head.

Rebecca propped herself up on her elbows as she leaned on the counter, "Oh you don't" she leaned down.

I frowned my face as I shook my head and gave her a very serious face, "Hell naw" I replied.

Rebecca started putting food away, I just sat and watched her as she cleaned the kitchen.

"Here you can take this for lunch or dinner tomorrow" she put some food in a container and slid it over to me.

I gave her a skeptical smirk, "Lemme find out" I replied as I peeked into the container.

Rebecca waved me off, "Boy please! Oh, that's right, you're a side dude, usually your chicks don't feed you. You betta stop messing with chicks that don't make sure you eat" she said as she closed the refrigerator and came back to the counter.

"But go head, finish telling me 'bout these *rules* you don't follow" she said motioning with her hands for me to continue talking.

I laughed as I sat at the counter. "Why you wanna know so bad? What you tryna make be my side thing" I asked trying to see where her head was in that matter.

"Rebecca Anabelle Matthews does not voluntarily share weinis nor will I be a rebound chick either" she banged the spoon on the side of the pot.

I choked back my juice, but some sprayed out of my mouth. I reached for a napkin to wipe up the mess.

I looked at Rebecca smirking at me.

"First of all, I don't know what kind of dudes you mess with but I ain't neva had a weinis. You really need to leave cornballs alone" I stated.

I laughed as I gulped down the last of my drink. "Second, what's your name again? Rebecca who?" I chuckled as she repeated her full name.

"Ok Ram, that's what Ima call you from now on, plus Rebecca sounds way too proper. Ya mom was like 'my baby gon get a good job' cause you're definitely not a Becky" we both laughed as she quickly joked on my name.

I looked at her as I was spinning from side to side in the chair. Our eyes met and her smile then her eyes turned really seductive...then my phone rang! *Dammit*!!

Chapter 8: Rebecca

'I'm in too deep like Jay Reid...'

I finally made it home and was settling in for the night when Levi alerted to being 'on his way' to pick up his car.

This man just gon keep coming around me smelling good enough to eat. I have not had sex in over two months, and lord knows I'm not tryna seem easy, but this man.

Thank God his phone rang because I was about to kiss him. As he was talking on the phone, I finished washing the pots and was drying my hands. I had listened to him talk for a few minutes and once I determined that it wasn't an important call, I decided to play with him for a lil bit.

I looked up at him and he winked his eye at me. I took that, along with him smelling like he was smelling as the green light.

I walked around the counter and told him to stand up. I smoothed out his shirt and I pushed him back into his chair. I took a deep breath, just inhaling him as I ran my lips across his neck without kissing him.

He looked down at me, "Whatchu doin?" he whispered as he held the phone away from his mouth.

I put my arms around his back, then placed my hands over his shoulders and just breathed him in again as I applied pressure to his collar. This time I kissed him on his neck. He moaned then closed his eyes.

"Ey Bruh gimme a minute" he hung up the phone.

He grabbed me by my hips and looked at me, then leaned in to kiss my neck as he squeezed my hips. It caused a moan to escape my lips.

"As much as I wanna take you down right now. I gotta be a gentleman" he sat up straight. "I promised my brother I'd be cool plus I dig you" he said.

I stood up and looked at him. I guess my face read *confused,* so he took my hand and placed it on his thigh then he slid my hand across his leg until I felt *it*!

It was so plump it made my vaginal walls throb. Gyrl, it is EVERYTHING I thought and more. Levi is working with something long and heavy, which made me want him more, even though he played me.

"Come on let's finish our talk" he said.

I looked at him. I'm ready NOW, and he wants to talk. Like sir, it's been over a month, why are we still talking? I thought to myself but decided to play along.

I nodded my head pretending not to be disappointed as I walked back to the other side of the counter by the sink. He smiled at me, "Ok so, we do it and then what?" he asked.

"I mean that's the bottom-line right?" I asked.

Levi shrugged while waiting for my response. He snickered at my serious disposition. "Pretty much" he replied.

"Look, this ain't my first time at this dance" I started to explain.

Levi interrupted me. "But it's your first-time dancing with me. Look, Ima always be real with you" Levi replied.

I nodded my head, "I respect that" I smiled as his phone started ringing again.

Levi silenced his phone and stood up, "Damn, so dig this here I gotta make a run real quick with my man but I want to say this, my name is good out here! You can ask about me! You'll never hear about me and some sucka shit in these streets" he shared.

I smiled at him. "Well, if you're already a known side piece who's 'on-call'..."

He cut me off again, "Listen, didn't I tell you I'm not a side dude nor do I follow 'side dude' rules? She comes when I call, she's more like my side" he motioned, and I laughed.

I switched my weight to my other leg, "Oh really, let me ask you a question. What if I want you but you're with her?" I asked.

"That depends" he looked down at me, wrapping his arms around my waist.

I pulled away from him, "Depends on what?" I asked very insulted at his response. *The hell you mean it depends!?!*

He pulled me back into his arms, but I kept my arms folded pretending to be about my business. Because truth be told. I didn't really care about any of that. We can really discuss that 'lata'. I wouldn't mind if he tossed me around a few different rooms. But I played mad when he asked me to look at him.

Levi squatted down so we were eye level, which made me laugh, "Nah for real come 'ere" he pulled me close to him.

I don't know why it took me this long to realize, this man really works out. He has abs and shit, I felt them. Damn, now I really don't care about whoever *her* is anymore.

"Look at me" I lifted my head to look him in his eyes. "It does depend though. It depends on where I'm at with you" he leaned down and kissed me. "It might not even be a *her* for you to worry about, do ya thang" he said as he walked away but backed up and kissed me again.

Sweet thangs let me tell you about that kiss...oh my god! My stomach drops just thinking about it. It was the softest, with the right amount of pressure at times, most breathtaking kiss I've ever had; it was like that heavy breathing and moaning while you're kissing type of thing.

Whew Chile, I pulled away, "I thought you had to make a run?" I asked.

He picked me up and sat me on the counter, "I do" he said as he kissed me again.

He kissed down my neck and softly bit the top part of my boobs. He pulled me flat on the counter. "What are you doing?" I objected because I knew he was tryna turn me up just to leave.

My fake thigh tightening meant nothing against these little bite things he kept doing. Oh, that shit drove me crazy. "Quit playin" I said as he massaged my legs.

"Who's playin" he replied and bit my thigh.

After finally giving in, this man inhaled down there and then he commenced to turning me all the way up. He kissed and sucked and licked and slurped and smacked my ass and nibbled me into a screaming fit, which ended with a quiet shake, almost like a vibration.

As if that wasn't tough, this jerk gon get up and say, "Lata, think about me" he announced.

Then kissed my forehead after washing his hands in the sink. I think I responded. A few minutes later I heard the door close.

In my mind I swung on myself like, "Bitch, you should know better" but as I laid in that moment feeling like I've never felt before, I really didn't care.

At least he aims to please! Nothing else even mattered at that point.

My alarm ringing woke me up. I looked around after catching myself from almost falling off the counter. My dumb ass really curled up and fell asleep on this counter.

I climbed off the counter and reminded myself to clean up the kitchen and walked back to my room.

I had to leave early because I had to meet Ant Peachy and get Brutus then go open the shop. I sent Levi a 'have a great day" message and stepped into the shower.

I had walked back in my room to see my phone was lit up, "I got a call and a message? What this boy done sent me?" I asked myself.

I clicked on the envelope to see a picture of Levi smelling his top lip with a caption, "I washed my face three times, and I can still smell you, see you lata" it read.

I shuddered at the thought of the orgasm I had the night before. That shit made my knees weak all over again. I sent him the eye wink and kiss face emoji then put the phone back on the charger.

Later that day...

I was walking Brutus down the block when Corey, MaJhonnie's ex rode past. I was so mad at myself for not thinking about giving him the finger until he was halfway up the block. I could not stand him. He cheated on Jhonnie, claimed it was once but then got not one but two chicks pregnant. Jhonnie tried to see "if the baby was his" because he swore it was not but then as we were waiting for the results, didn't another chick pop up claiming to be pregnant by Corey…the audacity!

That whole thing sent Jhonnie to Uncle Sammy's for over a month. I know she still talks to him sometimes. I know he told her he'd cover her mortgage payments for the last two months. I was checking the mailbox as Corey rode back past.

"Dammit, next time he rides by Ima give him the finger" I walked inside to lockup Jhonnie's shop. I guess she didn't tell him she's not coming back until next week.

I walked over to the elevator to get to the basement floor. I needed to go home. Once I got there, I fed Brutus and was about to warm up some leftovers when Levi's ringtone chimed. Yes, so what I already gave him a special ringtone.

I thought you forgot about me" I said answering the phone.

Levi laughed. "Never, whatchu doing?" he asked.

"Bout to find me something to eat" I said as I closed the refrigerator.

Levi started yelling at people in the background. "You eat seafood" he asked.

"Hell yea" I didn't mean to sound greedy, but I reacted too quickly.

Levi laughed then put me on hold.

I heard loud music and he asked me to 'give him thirty minutes' and hung up. I put the phone down, then did a backhand wave type gesture as I heated up my leftover lasagna and climbed into bed. *I'll mess around and starve waiting on him…*

An hour or so later a message came thru, "Don't go to sleep" it read.

I chuckled, "I'm so sleepy, I can't promise you I won't" I responded.

"Say no more!" he immediately text back.

I held my phone in my hand as I waited for him to say something else, but it never came. I laid there waiting; or so I thought until my phone vibrating scared me out of my sleep.

'Damn, why am I so sleepy today' I asked myself. I messed around and dozed off, my phone vibrated.

I opened the message envelope, "I'm outside" it read.

I rolled over to enter the code to disarm the lock. I text him back, "It's open, lock it behind you" I turned over to watch him on the camera walking off the elevator.

He walked in the apartment, carrying a backpack and a tin pan.

"I hope you don't mind" he said as he took off his bag, "I gotta meet my Pops on this side of town early in the morning" he said lifting the pan.

"I bought you a seafood platter from my brother Boy's spot. He put the pan in the fridge and walked back into the bedroom.

"Lemme find out you a grandmom, you in bed already" he said sitting down on the chair across the room.

Levi looked tired but managed to smile at me. He started taking his watch off. "You mind if I take a shower?" he asked.

I went to get up, but he stopped me, "Naw you good, I don't need anything just tell me which door" he said.
I pointed over to the door behind me, "Right there" I replied.

He walked around the room and he walked into my bathroom, "Ok Ball-in" he yelled loud as hell before grabbing the doorknob.

"My nephew been saying that shit all weekend just mad random with it" he put his hand to his mouth and yelled it again as he stepped inside the bathroom and closed the door.

I hurried up and hopped out of bed to change from my long sleeve gown to my cute tank top mini nightgown. I put on my barefoot sandals Jhonnie made for me. I sprayed my after-shower mist and was putting lotion on my arms, when I heard the water turn off.

I hurried up and climbed back in the bed and pretended to watch TV as I waited for him to open the door.

My dumb ass was really sitting there waiting for him to open the door because I *know* he smelled amazing. I heard the sink water turn on and off and then on again. Just as I was running out of patience, he opened the door. And just like I thought, as I inhaled the steam drenched in his shower gel residue that filled the air, he smelled sooooo yummy!

'Damn he smells so fucking good! Oh, my goodness, what an intoxicating aroma'

"You gettin real pretty for me ain't ya?" I sat and just breathed it in.

He looked at me through the mirror. "You see me? You like it?" he asked playfully.

I propped myself up on my elbows, "You ight" I waved my hand.

He chuckled at me. "Oh yea, I see somebody changed into something more entertaining, so who's really getting pretty" he turned and smiled at me.

I heard what sounded like my voice say, "Come 'ere…"

Chapter 9: Jhonnie

"Here we go wit' the bullshit..."

I had gone to visit Rafiq again during my stop through Brandi's, but that is a whole 'notha story for an entirely different day.

I had been home for a few days and was ready to leave and go back to be with him. Rafiq had been maintaining contact with me since I left. He keeps telling me about all these places he wants to take me too when I come down there. Every day he asks me about 'when I was coming back?'

It didn't take long before I jumped back in the swing of things at work. Rebecca had these cleaning people that did a great job on the house. I hired them; they'll start coming every other Saturday. I don't know where she found them, but I loved them.

I had a lot going on, but my best friend said she needed me. So, when Rebecca aka Begs called, I planned dinner for us. She was coming over to "have a serious conversation about something that would require drinks" she said when she called me earlier.

I hope she plans to stay because I'm not trying to fight this hoe at two in the morning, she always trying to drive somewhere drunk! I decided Ima take her keys when she first gets here. I refused to go through it with her, not another morning will I yank this girl over trying to stop her from driving somewhere intoxicated.

The last time I made her cry and I felt horrible afterwards because I knew she was going through some shit, feel me? But when my friend since elementary school swung on me and scratched my chin and neck, all that understanding went out the window. I lost it on her!!!

"Rebecca, what the fuck" I yelled before I grabbed her by jacket to get a good grip, then swung her into her car.

I threatened the lives of her and her future children as I banged her against her hood. Our girlfriends had to pry my fingers off of her. I didn't speak to her for weeks. I was just over her shit that night. I felt myself getting annoyed again, so I blew and wiped my invisible bang out my face in an effort to calm down.

'Whew chile' I said out loud coming back to the present moment. We are years past that night. She's my Becca aka Begs; I named her that because she's always asking me for something. And I'm her Tink, she made that name when my cousins told her she couldn't call me by my family name, Stink. It's our thing it's been going on for years and it works for us, you know?

I pulled our decorated wine glasses out of the dishwasher, dried them off then took some frozen grapes out of the freezer. I had just stood up when I heard my door chime.

"Begs" I yelled opening the cabinet for the bowls.

Rebecca walked in, "Awwww, you got our glasses they are so pretty, and you cooked too! For me? I thought we was gon' order?" she asked falling right into the drama.

I mean holding her chest, shoulders all high, head to the side and she even had tears in her eyes.

I rolled my eyes as I turned back to my twerk break in front of the open fridge as I looked for my container of scallops.

"I know it's been a while since we did our lunch BUT you were just here drinking out that same glass last Sunday" I said over my shoulder.

"And I cook ALMOST every day well every other at least".

Rebecca quickly put the bags on the counter, "Girl, shut up! You know you only cook from Sunday to Wednesday and your boos feed you for the rest of the week" she said.

I laughed as I turned around to cook. "I mean I had to make new friends, you all in love and shit" I said with a shrug.

I was cutting up the shrimp and scallops when Rebecca began pulling stuff out of her bag.

"Tink, look what I got you" she said.

I turned around and saw two green jars labeled, *Yup* in her hand. I put the knife down as I walked over to the sink to wash my hands.

"Begs, what the hell? This new dude got you smoking" Rebecca pulled out a cigar wrap and slid it across the counter.

"Begs? I mean forget the fact that you weren't even a smoker, but you carry it around now" I reached over and grabbed a jar.

I opened the jar and inhaled deep into the jar. It smelled familiar, "I've smoked this before" I said smelling it again.

Rebecca turned away from me and walked over towards the landing leading towards my sitting room, but she didn't step down she just stood at the landing and fidgeted. "Yeah, about that..." she said in a low tone.

I sipped my wine, "About what?" I asked.

Rebecca turned around and her eyes danced around the room as she played with the jars. The more she played with the jars, it made *me* pay more attention to them.

I looked at the jars again. "Wait a minute"

I snatched a jar out of Rebecca's hand, "These are from Lo, aren't they?" I asked.

I opened the top to smell it again, "Hell yeah, I knew I smoked this before" I closed the jar looking at my friend for answers.

Now I'm very curious as to what "*yeah...about that*" means especially since my best friend is standing in my kitchen holding bud that she got from the dude that ghosted me. Yeah, I needed to know what exactly, "that" was...

"So um, remember that time you went to Uncle Sammy's, the time I housesat for you, before I moved in for a little while" I leaned back in position as I folded my arms across my chest.

Just then the doorbell chimed...

I cut my eyes at Rebecca as I walked towards the door. "Who" I yelled as I walked up the stairs.

"It's Lo and my brother Levi" he yelled.

I paused and tried to gather myself. I back pedaled down the stairs, "Hold on" I yelled.

I walked into the kitchen to see Rebecca downing her drink, then quickly poured another. "Ok what the *fuck* Rebecca" I said pointing at the door.

She gulped down her drink, "Jhonnie you gotta believe me, it's soooo not what you think! I just want to say before you open that door, I'm so sorry for taking…"

My stomach dropped; I felt this unexplainable wave of anxiety flood my body. I looked at Rebecca it was like I was frozen in place, "What in the hell is going on Rebecca" I asked calmly cutting of her apology.

She took a deep breath and slowly backed towards the door, "Let me get Lo and 'em and they can explain" before I knew it, I jumped at Rebecca, but she managed to get away and ran up the stairs to the door.

"Oh, y'all cool now huh Rebecca" I yelled.

I was at the bottom waiting for her return as she unlocked the door. I ran into the kitchen and grabbed a knife off my counter.

I walked back in pointing it at the three of them, "Y'all think this is a game, don't fucking play with me" I warned. "I'm nice but ain't shit sweet about me, now what the *fuck*?" I yelled.

"Mr. Logan aka "Where the fuck you been" I snapped.

He put his hands up as he stepped to the side of the door. 'Jhonnie, Ion want no problems with you" he announced disappearing outside.

I looked at Rebecca who was nervously watching between me and the other side of the door.

"Jhonnie please let them explain" she pleaded.

I took a step back. "Them? Who the hell is them?" I had pointed the knife in Rebecca's direction as I waited for an answer.

Then I heard an older male voice from the other side of the door.

"MaJhonnie, can I please come in?" a male voice came from the other side of the door.

I tried to catch the voice, but it wasn't registering.

I nodded at Rebecca, "Who is that" I mouthed the words as she opened the door.

I investigated the face of a more mature Logan and another older version of Logan but with a shorter beard.

The more mature Logan was very handsome. I mean real 2020 Richard Roundtree old man swag. I blinked my eyes coming back to reality.

"Come in" I waved my hand.

He walked past Rebecca and down the stairs towards me, extending his hand. I placed the knife in his hand.

"I didn't want this; I was trying to shake your hand, but I'll take it" he laughed.

I apologized as I tried so hard to quickly bring my spirit in as I was taught to always respect my elders. I tried to take my eyes off the door, but I couldn't. I mean I tried to relax but it was hard because I still had no clue as to what the hell was going on.

I slowly looked over at 'Mr. Logan Sr. sir' as he called my name pulling my attention away from Rebecca and Logan.

"Can we sit down and talk?" he asked.

I looked over into my sitting area and extended my hand, "Please, after you Mr. Logan Sr, sir" I extended my hand.

He turned to the door and mumbled something to Rebecca, the older version of Logan and the real Logan, then they all walked outside.

I walked into the room and sat on my chair leaving the other chair open for him. He immediately started his spiel.

"Listen I know you've only met me that one time, but I want to let you know, Logan thinks very highly of you. He did nothing but talk about you for months. I don't want you to be angry at him for his avoidance. I just needed to be sure..."

I took a deep breath, "No offense *Mr. Logan Sr, sir* but," he cut me off.

"You can call me Dean for now" he advised.

I nodded my head. "I'm still trying to understand why my best friend is apologizing right before Lo knocks at my door, this bout to be some bullshit" I covered my mouth, "I'm so sorry" I quickly apologized.

He waved it off laughing at my apology.

Then it finally clicked in my head what he had just said, "Wait, what do you mean, you had to be sure? Sure, of what" I turned to face him.

"What if I told you that I told Lo he couldn't date you?" Dean sat back in his seat, then crossed his ankle across his knee.

I cocked my head back in confusion, "Excuse me" I asked pushing down other choice words.

Dean grabbed my hand and looked into my eyes, "Not because there's something wrong with you. You're an amazing young lady but I can't have my baby son dating his older sister" the whole room grew warm and wavy then it all turned black.

Sister? Wait, sister? How I'm an only child?

My father died when I was away at school.

This just didn't make sense…

How could Lo possibly be my brother? I questioned the validity of his statement.

My mother told me that her and my dad married when they were just kids. It doesn't make sense.

Nope! Shaft is lying, I don't have a brother and if I did, it damn sure ain't Logan Murphy.

I stared at the lines in my hands for a little bit until Dean pulled me from my thoughts again. "Did you hear me?" he asked.

I shook my head, so he repeated, "Your mother and I dated off/on for a short time many years ago when I was married to a lady named Estelle, and I knew your mother. But your mother" he paused.

I looked up at him, "Did you know my father?" I asked.

He smiled at me, "Of course I do, I am your father" he said jokingly.

"Well did you know my *Dad*" I asked annoyed.

"I will say this, Stanley was a stand-up dude, never had a problem with him. So, I can respect him enough to say, Yes, he was your Dad, I won't take that from him. But I think you should know, he died knowing the truth" he slid a bag forward with his foot then picked it up and set it between us.

"I have been trying to talk to your *mother*. First time, when Stu first got sick, and rumors started swirling that he might not be your biological father. Celeste was evasive, so I just kinda watched you from a distance, I always had questions because um, well it's complicated" he said rubbing his face. "Then I lost track of you when she left town" he shared.

"I came again after Stu died with some questions. Your mom refused me, saying you didn't need any more stress" he reached inside the bag and picked up an envelope.

I jumped up from my seat and excused myself, "I'm sorry but I need to call my mom" I walked into the room to get a huge gulp of my wine and find my phone.

I heard steps behind me, but I couldn't turn to look so I just held my head up as I stood in front of my sink looking out the window. The view was getting blurrier and blurrier as I blinked tears down my face.

Logan cleared his throat, "You okay Jhonnie, I know this is crazy!" he said.

I sipped my water. "Yeah, so now I guess it's cool for you and my best friend huh" I smirked at Logan as he walked over to me.

"I mean, if you are my sister, technically I am fair game" he smiled as he leaned up against the counter. "But naw, I wouldn't do that to you" he tapped the counter.

I looked over my shoulder at him and he smiled which finally made me break down. Logan came around and pulled me into a hug, "Come on man with all this crying Jhon you're too tough for this" he squeezed then hugged me.

I pushed off his chest, "So is that why you ghosted me? You bastard" I laughed as I wiped my face then rubbed his shirt knowing it creeped him out.

Logan hated for anyone to be touchy when he's wearing white but when I wiped my tears and then touched his shoulder. Logan just put his hands in his pockets and shrugged it off.

"Yeah Maann, my bad for that. You have no idea how much shit I woulda heard if I even answered your calls before my pops had a chance to talk to your mom" Logan said, quickly reminded me, I was supposed to be calling my mother.

I had walked over to the counter to open the wine bottle, "My mom? Wait so does my mom know about you?" I asked.

Logan nodded his head and pushed in the stool.

"Yeah, everybody supposed to come to my brother Lance well Pudd's house for 'Dunch' in two Sundays" he said.

I turned my head, "Who's everybody?" I asked.

Logan clapped his hands, "Er'body, my brova's, pops, my Mi-Mi, some cousins and shit! You, you're invited; Becs and your moms" he shared.

"My mom, she already confirmed this *dunch*?" I shook my head in disbelief.

I flipped thru some drawers in my kitchen then looked at Logan.

"I know you got something already rolled that I can smoke, not now but you know...now*ish* " I walked over to take the lids off my candles on the counter.

Logan laughed, "Hell yeah I do" he pulled a blunt from behind his ear and lit it before he handed it to me.

I snatched it from him, "Not with ya dad here" I put it out and fanned the air. "You gotta let the candles work first" I hurried up and lit them.

Logan fell over laughing as he jogged to the hallway. "Ayo Pop, Jhonnie said she wanna smoke but she's scared too...in front of you" he looked back smiling at me.

I stomped my foot at him as my phone rang. It was my mother calling me back.

Dean walked into the kitchen, "This is your spot, you do ya thing!" he instructed.

I excused myself and walked into my studio to talk to my mother. Of course, she offered no explanation except Stanley was my Daddy and Dean was nobody I needed to know at that time. We had a heated exchange which resulted in me hanging up the phone.

I walked into the kitchen, right over to the blunt that was on the counter where Logan left it. I picked it up and lit it. Dean walked over next to me, he placed an envelope and a small box on the counter.

He touched my shoulder, "I'm always ready to talk whenever. I hope you can join us for family dunch to meet the rest of the family" he said then stepped back.

I took a long drag and dropped my head back between my shoulders and blew the smoke in the air.

"This is crazy" I shook my head.

I looked over at Dean, "So let me get this straight, you're not only my biological father but you're also the father of the dude that dated me for a couple months then ghosted me after his party, only to show up here after tryna hook up with my best friend" I said.

Logan scoffed. "Damn, it does sound fucked up when you put it like that" he chuckled.

He quickly stopped laughing as I cut my eyes at him. "Yeah, but I'm not the one" he raised his hands as Dean looked at him confused.

Logan shook his head and flagged his hand, "My bad, pay me no mind" he waved his hands in the air.

Dean touched the envelope again, "Please take these next few days to consider the possibilities. I really want to talk to you. I hope to hear from you" he said softly.

I propped myself up on the edge of the counter as I crossed my legs in front of me, "I can't make any promises" I replied.

Dean nodded his head and walked towards the door. Logan kept adjusting his hat as he tried to find the words, but I flagged him off, "Go head, it's cool" I waved.

He snapped his fingers, gave me a peace sign, then left, "Ima holla atchu Jhonnie" he yelled before he closed the door.

A few minutes later, Rebecca scary ass came peeking around the corner, "Can I come back in" I looked over at her as I closed my eyes letting the wine sit on my tongue before I swallowed it.

I sucked my teeth hard, "Not until you tell me exactly what yo ass was apologizing for" I said sharply.

Rebecca stepped further into the kitchen, "I ain't want you yanking me thinking I was messing with Ghostbastard" she sat at the counter finally taking off her jacket.

"I was saying sorry for what they were about to tell you" she looked at me with her saddest eyes. "So, girl, please tell me you saw Levi" she said with a huge smile.

I picked up my glass. "Who the hell is Levi" I asked watching Rebecca grow with excitement as she described him.

She kept repeatedly saying, "Oh my goodness', Tink you looked right at him" she replied in a disappointed tone.

Finally, she pulled out her phone, "Levi is, well one of y'all older brothers" she hands me the phone showing a pic of four grown men that all favor Dean but had their own separate swag and it was turned all the way up, according to these pictures.

I snatched the phone, "What the..." I stared at the screen.

I had never seen men more beautiful. "These are *my* brothers?" I asked moving through her pictures.

Rebecca proudly nodded her head.

"So how long have you known" I asked handing her back the phone.

"Yeah, about that..." she put her head down.

I threw the cork from the wine bottle at her, "Bitch, don't play" my voice was hard.

She looked at me, "Fine, remember that night I told you about when me and Neesh went to the bar" I thought for a minute then yelled, "That was in July!! You mean like almost six months ago, July" I yelled.

Rebecca shook her head then covered her face. "I said I was sorry, they wanted to talk to your mom to be sure before they told you, but she kept playing around with meeting Dean. I didn't know how bad it was until your mom called me asking for my help" she said and tried to keep talking.

I cut her off and started banging on the counter, 'What the fuck do you mean my mother called you...WHEN" I yelled with my palm facing up waiting for her response.

Rebecca stepped back from the counter, "The month before last" she flinched jokingly and all I could do is glare at her until tears rolled down my face.

I thought about all the times I protected Rebecca from her own family. I thought about the night I was almost taken to lock-up for beating up Rebecca's cousin's *girlfriend*, and after all of the things my mom has done, you helped her hide something from me...but that's a whole notha story for an entirely different day.

Now, Rebecca rode for me too, but I guess hearing that she held this for nearly six months blew me away, all I could do is wipe my face.

"Well, can I at least tell you what I found out about Logan?" she asked.

I scoffed as I thought about what her inside investigation would reveal.

I quickly let her know that we could compare notes. "Chile please, you think when he ghosted me, I didn't put my ear to the ground about him" I poured some frozen grapes into my wine glass. "I just stopped caring when I saw Fiki again" I shrugged.

Rebecca's eyebrows went up, "Well hell whatchu find out" she pulled out her stool, grabbing a shot glass, she pushed the wine glass away, "Uhn uh, keep that cutesy stuff I need a hard drink!"

I poured her a shot.

"Ok, wait so let me take this time to apologize again. I honestly just didn't know how to tell you" Rebecca's face was wrecked with emotion.

I shrugged, "You could have just told me like 'Tink listen, there is nothing wrong with you!!! Girl, that boy is your brother'...and then *we* could have moved on from there" I sipped my wine then looked at her trying to contain my disappointment.

"Rebecca, you know what I went thru trying to figure out what was wrong with me and what went wrong with Lo! Especially after all that shit with Corey" I took a very much needed deep breath.

Rebecca looked at me like a sad puppy while nodding her head.

"Or you could have said, 'You know how you always say your mom got some shit with her? But it's cool, I definitely get it" I pointed at her then hit the counter.

I held my hands up in a surrender motion pretending not to want to fight, even though I really did so I said it being facetious hoping to start something.

Rebecca went right for it. "What do you mean, 'you get it'" Rebecca threw her shot back then slammed her glass down waiting for my response.

I smirked at her irritated face, "I get that you sold me out because you were tryna keep fucking my brother, not Lo, the other one. What's his name, Levi?" I snapped and pointed at her.

Rebecca tried hard not to laugh. Do you know this tramp looked me dead in my face and said, "Ok, so if you know that then why are we fighting, as opposed to you letting me tell you about how much I think I love ya brother because he is a whole PROBLEM!! That's a much better story" she smiled at me.

I busted out laughing at her excited face, "Wait a minute, so Levi is the 'new dude' you've been telling me about?" I finally concluded.

Rebecca threw another shot back, "Gurrlll, now you understand my dilemma, when they said I couldn't tell you I told them, 'y'all are on borrowed time" Rebecca slid the blunt out the ashtray and relit it.

I slapped my hand against the counter in total shock, "So you smoke now, first you're secretly sleeping with 'my brother" I stopped to think I liked how that sounds...*my brother.*

I smiled but quickly returned to my point. "And then you tell me about it as we blow it in the air?" I was so confused.

Who was this girl standing in front of me? No judgement but I needed to know, "What the hell happened...how did they get to you" she took a deep breath and told me how it all went down.

"Well, one day I was downtown shopping..."

Rebecca left my house for the second time this week and it was only Wednesday. I knew I had to get myself together. Especially since my mother called me twice while I was talking to Rebecca.

"Finally," I said as I pressed her name and the phone started ringing.

"Mom" was all I could get out before emotions flooded me and I wept on the phone to my mother.

"Mom, he wasn't my father? Why didn't you tell me?" I asked.

Through her tears my mother told me how Dean was living a very different life and he wasn't good for me.

"Me being grown, wanting him I got pregnant with you. But Dean was with Estelle so we couldn't be together. Your Dad's family was no longer in the game or making illegal money so. Stanley was safe for me, so we got together, I had you and he married me" she sniffed. "And that was that" she finished.

I couldn't believe my mom was telling me this story. "Did Daddy know before he died that I wasn't his daughter" my mom was quiet. "Hello" I repeated my last question.

She sniffed "Yes he knew, Stanley couldn't have children and he was absolutely fine with it because he wanted a family with me" she explained.

I cried even harder. I loved that man and that man really loved me. I knew it even more in that moment.

My mom apologized in her usual way, "Jhonnie I can't go back and fix this for you, so let's just move on. You asked a question and I'm giving you an answer, all you need to know is…Dean is your father. Oh, and you have four brothers. So, no you're not an only child but you're still my one and only. So, are we good?" she asked very nonchalantly.

I took a deep breath, helping myself to move on and blew out hard, "So you're going to this thing next Sunday" my mom confirmed and asked me to reconsider.

I told her I'd think about it and ended the call. I declined the last two *dunch* invitations. A whole month passed since they dropped the bombshell on me, so of course everyone is on my ass to attend this *'dunch'*.

I can do without it...so I planned to git!

I called Rafiq but he didn't answer. I decided to practice the technique Amira taught me called, "Down the drain". I gathered my things and walked into the bathroom for a cleansing. I had just come out of the shower and was putting on my body butter when Rafiq called me back.

"Whassup Beautiful" he asked smiling at me.

I forced a smile as he gave a cheesy smile into the camera while he combed his beard.

"I miss you" I said smiling at him.

He leaned into the phone, "Whatchu say, no you don't" he kept looking in the screen like he was searching for something. "What happened, what's wrong?" he asked.

I wiped a tear from my face, "My mom wants me to meet my father and the rest of my family next Sunday. Clearly there's an incentive for her" I explained my mother's nature to Rafiq.

Rafiq put me on hold then came back in the frame. We talked a little more before he had to end the call.

I eventually drifted off to sleep, I was not looking forward to the next day...

The next day at work was just as hard as I thought it would be.

But receiving a pink rose bouquet with a sunflower from Rafiq made it all better.

"Oh, well then who are these from?" Rebecca asked walking in with another bouquet of yellow roses and violets.

I read the card, "I should have known" I laughed as I read the card out loud, "Stay pretty from Ms Shug and 'nem" I put those on my kitchen island.

"I thought Rafiq did, but I think his mom and Godmom sent them, either way it made my day" I picked up my pink bouquet to take it upstairs for my room.

Rebecca danced, "Awww, look at us! We both got Boos at the same time" I came back into the kitchen.

"Um Rafiq and I are just friends" I said trying to convince myself more than anyone else.

Rebecca gave the most sarcastic laugh as she lit my candles. "Which reminds me, I got some more orders for you" I nodded my head as I lit our smoke.

"I'm going to do a new massage candle" I said.

Rebecca threw her fist in the air like she won something, "Yeesss, I want it" she took the blunt and sat at the counter.

"Sooooo" Rebecca pulled the chair out and got in position.

"So, what" I looked up at her from the *empanadas* that I was trying to perfect.

"Tell me about this *'friend'* Rafiq" she said while doing air quotes.

I caught myself trying not to blush. "Uh huh, we're just *friends*" she mocked me.

I inhaled and then cut my eyes over at her while.

I snapped my fingers, "Bitttccchhhh" I exhaled as I fell against the counter.

"Ok Rafiq, used to be...okay...okay...okay..." I waved my hands like I was erasing my first thought.

"There's Rafiq, then there's Fiki *and* I recently was introduced to Ski. Girl, I want Ski" I clapped my hands and went to the sink. "I mean don't get me wrong, Rafiq can get it all by himself, I mean you seen him, he looks good" I shared with my friend.

Rebecca grunted her agreement as she was drinking her cucumber water.

"I don't know what happened in the last six, maybe seven years but Rafiq used to be a real chubby boy, like 'I know you got something to eat in this car' type big boy" I said.

Rebecca stopped me from talking. "That man that was on your video chat used to be chubbier than he is now because Jhonnie we know you like 'em plump but" she bit into a piece of fruit.

I giggled because it was true. I'm 5'10 I can't do nothing with a little guy, I don't like sloppy fat, but I do love a chubby boy.

"Well, this Rafiq, is solid and he has a lil stomach, but I think that shit is cute" I declared.

Rafiq has to be about 6'0, he's light brown skin with a big bushy beard. He has a neat, dark Caesar haircut with these perfect eyebrows and a chipped tooth. Oh, and he has a scar over his eye so it looks like how when back in the day the boys would put the three cuts in the eyebrow? Well, his is natural.

"Girl, and all the bitches in the town want him. So, you already know how that goes" I said twisting my lips.

Rebecca laughed "So is he, you know because I think mine is, well not mine but his family, well your family is" I looked at Rebecca in confusion.

"Wait, what the hell are you saying?" I asked.

Rebecca slapped the countertop. "Ok, girl yes, your family, your brothers, cousins, yo uncles and maybe yo daddy"

I interrupted her, "My father" I corrected her.

Rebecca acknowledged and offered apologies.

"But yeah, your father was like 'that guy', your brothers with I believe the exception of *my* Levi, only because in all this time, I've never seen him engaged in it like I've seen Lo...or Boy. Hell, I know Pudd moves around a lot out of the area with his herbal goodies" she finished and sipped her water.

I looked at Rebecca questionably. She saw my face and laughed, "Girl I be in it! I play sleep when they be at the house" she dipped her empanada into a sauce and bit into it. "Ooo and something always slips at Dunch" I dropped some more empanadas in my deep fryer.

So, my brothers are drug dealers. Solid, I mean why wouldn't I belong to a drug dealing family. That's what's been missing from my life. It has been drama filled since the age of fifteen.

"Oh my god, that's what I've been missing, 'First Lady of a drug dynasty" I joked, and Rebecca played along.

"Now what the hell is this Family Dunch gon be about?" I asked.

Rebecca explained how they started with a brunch, but they could never get there until like three o'clock, so Pudd switched the time and started calling it 'Dunch" she did the air quote gesture.

"Girl, the food" she threw her head back and kicked her feet like an excited child. "The food is amazing. Levi makes a to-go pan for us to eat off of for the next few days" I looked at her excitement.

I smiled and nodded. Rebecca picked up on my shade pointing to her thick thighs, "Bitch, fuck you! Yes, I gained a few pounds but I'm happy" I laughed at her.

"And I'm happy for you" I walked around the counter and hugged her. "I'm just noticing some things" I said as she hugged me back.

"Can you please come to Dunch; they've been planning this one for months. All your brothers got you gifts! Your grandmom will be there...oh I love Ms Mi-Mi" she dropped her shoulders while holding her chest.

I looked at Rebecca. "Oh, you in *in* huh" she laughed and hugged me.

"Come on, this is perfect, you're my best friend! What are the odds I'd be in love with your brother?" she asked.

I nodded my head at the irony of it all. "I definitely didn't *saw* this coming. Especially since I was raised as an only child, by a man that biologically didn't make me, but hey, I just found all of this out at twenty-four so hell anything is possible" I raised my glass.

Rebecca hugged me tight. "Well, I'm your sister" she squeezed me before pulling back.

"You had a great Dad! He made sure you had a good life and honestly Tink you lived; we lived a very sheltered life" I laughed at Rebecca's new street credibility.

"I know I just can't believe it; do you know he knew I wasn't his daughter all that time" Rebecca wiped my face with a napkin.

"Really, see that makes him even doper than I thought" she said.

I stood up and walked back to the stove. "I know" I smoothed my hair up.

"I don't know about this whole 'dunch family thing" I poured myself more wine. I relit our smoke and looked at Rebecca. "So, what's in it for you?" I asked.

She looked at me. "In it for me?" she put her hands on her chest.

I lifted my glass, "No offense Begs but you don't get to act like you're solely down with me, you've been dating my brother and around *my* family for months behind my back. Shit, damn near a year...so yeah, I have to ask" I paused holding my glass to my lips.

Rebecca nodded in agreement. "You got that, but to be honest, all I want is your blessing to be with your brother" she said looking at me.

I sipped my wine as I leaned against the counter, thinking before I gave my blessing, "Since you are dating my brother, you *gotta* clean up your shit" I pulled on my blunt then continued my point.

"Because you know how I am about my boy cousins but now I have *real* brothers?" I scoffed and looked at Rebecca with my lips twisted and my eyebrow raised.

I can't wait to slap a hoe over my brother...I like how that sounds!

"You're my friend and I love you so don't say you weren't warned mm kay? I will beat you the fuck up for real" I blew out. "So, clean it up!" I ordered.

"I *did*" she whined.

Rebecca wasn't the type to date one guy. I looked at her impressed at her willingness to empty her roster.

"Alright because if you fuck my brother over like you've done some of ya others...you heard what I said right I?" I asked.

Rebecca put her hand up to stop me from saying it.

"No really, we had that talk and I told him, 'if I cut off my hoes and this don't work out...you gon owe me some hoes" she said with the straightest face.

After I got myself together from the laugh fit, I just had around my kitchen, I looked at Rebecca, "Now if he's doing him, dontchu' be no fool, just don't put your hands on him" I warned. Rebecca can get real handsy sometimes.

I refilled my glass, "I must say I want to meet this Levi...now! Call him" I pushed her phone over.

Chapter 10: Leviathan

'Man, this ain't my table...'

I was getting off the exit to meet up with Logan when Ram called. "Video for real" I pressed the button and I saw Ram high ass smiling. "What's up Babe? Who you smoking with?" I asked.

I heard someone yell, "Hi Brother" then Jhonnie comes into the screen all cheesy.

"Heeeyyy" I replied. She made me smile big as hell.

"Where y'all at" I turned my attention back to the road.

"Can you come by Jhonnie's real quick?" Ram pushed Jhonnie out of the picture.

I had to look at Ram to be sure she was serious. She knew the plan, Pop wanted us to meet Jhonnie together but more importantly my Mi-Mi wanted to meet her first.

I did not have to say anything before Rebecca started explaining, "I know but now she's saying she's not sure if she's coming to 'dunch', so I'm calling in for reinforcements" she giggled.

"Come on man, look Lo bout to get in" I said as I pulled onto Lo's block.

Jhonnie yelled, "Noooo I just want to meet you please don't tell that bastard nothing, please" she pleaded.

I looked at the clock and looked up to see Lo coming out of his front door. "Here he come, alright lemme make this run with him and Ima hit you back" I ended the call just as Logan opened the door.

"My man" he shook my hand before handing me an envelope.

"Pop said tell you to do what y'all talked about" he said.

I took the envelope and put it in my visor, "Pop here" I looked around for his car.

"Naw I saw him earlier at Mi-Mi's" he explained his day.

I pulled away from his house. "I must've just missed yall, I took Mi-Mi to the market earlier."

Logan put his hands on my shoulder, "Good look on that I couldn't do that market run no more" he shook his head.

"You're crazy, Mimi be hooking me up with food all the time" I laughed at him.

Logan objected, "Uhn uh Mimi be tryna get you to eat that healthy stuff" he shook his head.

I laughed at my brother, "That's because you're used to eating out" I joked.

Logan flagged me off, "Maaann, I'm not tryna hear that! You just stopped coming to the bar for dinner" he fired back.

He was right ever since I've been with Ram, between her and Mimi I don't worry about food. "It's like every time I see them, they are sending me home with a bag saying, 'bring my dish back!"

I laughed remembering the time Ram went off on a whole rant because I brought her back the wrong bowl. I switched up the bags by mistake. Then, Mi-Mi refusing to return Rebecca's bowl, didn't go over too well. I ended up having to buy her a new set for that one bowl. Mimi asked for the set, I made Boy buy it to get back in her good graces.

I tapped Logan's arm, "So yo, I gotta throw a curve ball in our plans tonight, I gotta do something for Ram" I shared as I drove to our next destination.

Logan threw his hands up and dropped them loudly on his lap.

"Come on man, you're supposed to be *my man*! You've been shaky lately bruh" he said in a serious tone.

I heard my little brother loud and clear. I *had* been cancelling on him a lot these past few months.

"I am your man, I'm also a couple otha folks' guy' too! But I hear you and I gotchu, I need tonight" I pleaded.

Logan waved me off, "I ain't no hater, so handle ya business but Ima need you to tighten it the fuck up" he said getting out of the car.

I told Logan I loved him as he opened the door.

"You already know" Logan said as he shook my hand then pulled me in for a hug. "Just hold me down until Tyreem get here" he requested.

I nodded my head, "Naw I'm here witchu I just can't do the last part" we walked inside the spot and Logan shook hands with this guy that led us to an office.

"This bet not be no bullshit" Logan said right before this Hector looking guy walked in smiling too much. Logan looked at me and we both said it with our eyes, 'It's 'bout to be some bullshit!'

Logan took off his hat and we sat down.

After leaving Logan, I called Ram's phone but got her voicemail. I called her again, still no answer. It was almost eleven o'clock, she might be sleep. I pulled off the exit heading to Jhonnie's house anyway.

I got to the house and her lights were still on. As I was walking up the sidewalk, the door opened.

Jhonnie came onto the porch as she wrapped her sweater around herself. "Come up this way" she waved me over.

"MaJhonnie...heeyyy I'm Levi" she smiled as I walked up the stairs and hugged her.

We walked in the house. Ram was sleeping on the chaise.

"She's been sleep for a minute" Jhonnie pointed as she walked by. I followed her into the kitchen, "Do you want something to drink" she asked.

I nodded, "Juice please" she poured me a glass as I sat at the countertop.

"Oh, you like this juice too huh, Ram put me onto this" I asked causing her to scoff loudly at me.

"I'm the one who put Rebecca onto it, so you're welcome" she said as she slid the glass over.

She leaned on the counter and looked at me, "So, what's your deal" she asked in a very direct tone.

I looked at her, "Huh" I asked being caught off guard.

She didn't miss a beat. "I'm not even talking about the whole *brother* thing, what are you doing with my friend?" she asked.

I nodded my head, "Ohhh, naw that's my baby" I smiled as Jhonnie stood up never taking her eyes off me.

We chopped it up for a minute about some other stuff, I realized we had a few mutual friends. Her cousin Rhyon is tight with one of my close homies, I would see him from time to time. Real cool dude but not a person you can ask too many questions about too many things.

Jhonnie laughed, "So I fly nearly four hours away to come back and meet my brother at the airport, that lived two towns over from me for pretty much my whole life" I thought about what she said, and it was crazy how they met.

Lo had seen Jhonnie at a few parties over this one weekend when he went to visit his homeboys out of town. Then when they ended up on the same flight, he almost missed his chance because he thought she was a narc.

I laughed as I sat in her kitchen smoking, I laughed at my brother's paranoia. Jhonnie was a calm smoker because you wouldn't know it just looking at her. Couple things I left knowing, my sister was very pretty, and she was about her shit. Oh, and she damn sure wasn't a narc.

"So, are you coming?" I asked getting up from the chair.

She shrugged her shoulders, "I don't know, my mom is stressing me out about it" I laughed at the thought of Ms Celeste. I wondered if Jhonnie looked inside her box.

"Yeah, she's a piece of work" I tapped the counter as I walked away. "So, I did my part, we gon see you next week right" I asked before I walked up the stairs to the front door.

Jhonnie followed me into the hallway, "Maybe, you not gon take ya boo-thang witchu?" she asked pointing in the room.

I looked at Ram bundled up on the chaise sleeping. "Nah, I don't feel like that fight tonight" I replied feeling exhausted from the thought.

Jhonnie laughed understanding my pain.

She walked me up the stairs and opened the door, "I'll come on one condition" she stated.

"Oh my god! Another condition come on man" I shook my head as I played like I'd been pushed forward.

She folded her arms and lifted her chin. I took a deep breath, "What is it" I asked leaning against the door.

She leaned against the wall, "Why is my mother so on board with all of this, why now? What am I not being told?" she asked.

Dayum!! I almost made it out without getting in the middle of this shit. But if we were going to be family then it's best that I keep it real with her.

"On some real shit, from what I'm hearing, money" I shrugged at her.

Her face didn't even seem surprised. "I fucking knew it" she reached over and unlocked her screen door.

"Last question, when did you find out about me?" she asked.

"I found out about you possibly being my sister, like a lot of our family did" I shared with her.

She stepped back and raised her eyebrows, "And when was that?" she asked skeptically.

I opened the door and stepped outside, "at Lo's party" I held onto the door.

"When your Dad snatched Lo away right before he asked for a birthday kiss" she covered her mouth and held the door open.

"Wow, see grownups ain't shit sometimes, now I'm out here bout to date my half-brother because folks just lying, ugghhh" she waved it off as she closed the door. "Bye Brother" she snapped.

I played back what Jhonnie said about 'parents lying' that shit is crazy. And now that I really think about it, Jhonnie is only younger than me by a few months. So, Pops was cheating on my moms for a minute, 'I thank God she's not here to see this mess unfold I turned on my music and zoned out.

Next Sunday can you hurry up and get here?

Chapter 11: Bop

'I'm the shake-up...'

Logan's birthday season was here, and I was so glad to be going home. For the last two months, whenever he called me; that was all he talked about, his party. Oh, and random stories about a chick he met coming back from seeing me in my new condo. He flew out for our homie Coddy, that had just come home from his five-year bid.

"Wait until you meet her Bop, she's bad" I drove along towards the bar to meet up with the crew on my visit in town.

"Oh, she's coming to your party?" I asked Logan.

He replied with such pride in his face. I pulled into the parking lot, spotting everybody's ride "Levi's here, and there goes Pudd car" I pointed out as I backed into a spot closer to the door. This was a pre-party at the bar to his big party weekend.

Lemme back up to give you some history, I met Logan and the Murphy's when his aunt Denita aka Ant Neet and my mom became friends when Logan and I were young boys.

His grandmother: or rather Mi-Mi, used to watch me when we were about two. Logan and I clicked over PB&J sandwiches one summer, and we've been brothers ever since.

Honestly, I don't remember not knowing them. Mi-Mi has pictures of me dressed up with the other cousins for church, Easter, birthday parties, Christmas, you name it. I was there.

Naturally, I thought we were family, we were close cousins that were always together. I think I was in junior high when I found out we weren't really related. It was at my grandpa's funeral.

Not being blood did not change a thing with us though, we was tighter than tight from that day on.

We walked into the bar and Lo lit up. "Oh shit, she came Bop" he tapped my arm as he walked over towards the same girl I'd been hoping to see.

Get the fuck outta here, her?!

She was so beautiful. Even prettier than I remembered. I loved everything about her. She's taller than your average woman but still small enough in comparison to me *and* she was very nicely proportioned. She wore her hair up with black frame glasses.

I think I stopped breathing on the low when she looked at me and smiled. I had to turn away.

She has these chubby cheeks; her eyes were beautiful. They were brown, but I loved how they were shaped. She had perfect teeth with a pretty ass smile, just like I remembered.

Logan waved me over. "Jhonnie, this is my brother Bop. Bop, this is Jhonnie" I extended my hand.

I quickly looked away, breaking eye connection with Jhonnie. "Oh, and these are my other brothers Levi and Lance" they waved as they walked over.

We all greeted her and then gave them privacy. Levi pointed to the bar and I nodded my head. We ordered our drinks as we scanned the room.

"So whatchu' think?" Levi asked.

I tried to play it cool but Pudd must have picked up on the vibe. "I think Bop got his shovel out for the young lady. You see how he was looking at her" he said with a smile.

I laughed as I sipped my drink. He put his hand to his ear, "Huh? I didn't hear any objection" Pudd laughed as he walked towards the kitchen.

I kept my thoughts to myself and pushed on past that last comment. I turned around and just watched her from across the room.

MaJhonnie huh? I smirked and sipped my drink.

Looking at her took me back to seventeen when I first saw her. She was pretty as hell, a real down girl. I made that conclusion when she without hesitation fought some guys that was trying to fight her boy cousin *and stood* tall with 'em.

I remember watching her walk away after she put her purse around her back. I thought about her for some time after that. I would always just think of her and what I'd say if I ever saw her again.

Imagine my disappointment when I learned this girl that I met so long ago turned out to be one of my homie's close cousins. That automatically made her off limits, and now she's standing here as my brother, my best friend's future *I don't know,* but I knew she was definitely off limits.

Dayummmm, maybe she's got a sister. I sipped my drink as I tuned back into Levi's conversation about his crazy ass ex, Tina.

Damn, she is so fucking beautiful...I couldn't stop looking at her.

I turned back to look at her, but she moved. *Where'd you go?* I thought scanning the room.

"Soooo, who's Bop" she asked from behind me. I turned around and smiled at her.

"I dunno" I muttered as I shrugged. "Never knew your real name was MaJhonnie" I raised my eyebrow.

She turned around to put her back to the bar, "Shut up, you had to know that wasn't my name, but no really…how the hell do you know Lo?" she asked.

I cleared my throat at Logan coming over, "You heard him, Lo is my brother. Enjoy your night, Stink" I raised my cup as I walked away.

There's a story behind that…we'll get into that later.

Surprisingly, Logan and Stink had been kicking it. According to Logan, he wasn't chilling with hardly any of his usual chicks. I remember him telling me how he had deleted some of the chicks out of his phone.

We were out to dinner during his visit out West before his party and he decided to share his feelings.

"I think Jhonnie could be the one, but I don't know Bop" was how he started the conversation.

I looked up from the menu. "What don't you know?" I asked him.

He shrugged. "I dunno its weird, like she's sexy right but when we're chilling that's just what it is. Real chill, but not in a bad way, it's just not sexual" he explained.

I put the menu down to look at him, "You mean like y'all ain't never" I asked joining my hands together.

"Dawg, not even a kiss, crazy right?" Logan shook his head.

I was shocked but kinda happy on the low that they hadn't gone the sexual route, which means they're not *that* serious. But this ain't like Lo, he usually loses interest after a few weeks, especially without sex. I decided to not push the issue though.

"What shoes you wearing for the party" I asked changing the topic.

"Aww man, you're not ready" Logan said stretching.

I shook my head as I patted his shoulder, "Listen here young man!"

I took a deep breathe and gave him sympathy vibes, "I don't want to upstage you at your own shit so I suggest you come hard" I said rubbing my hands together.

"Don't think it's gon be just another corny black suit with some dumb shit on my feet" I wiped down my arm.

Logan flagged his hand, "Bop, look at me. Do I look worried? Because I'm not" he said drinking his water.

We continued talking over our meal.

The party was finally here, I had flown in town early for Logan's party. I lowkey really couldn't wait to see her. She told Logan she was going to see her other family, so I went to the block, but she wasn't there. I *wanted* to see her bad.

Finally, we started getting ready to meet up for the get together before the party.

I remember the night of the party, MaJhonnie walked in with this black fitted dress that came to her knees and her sleeves were long, but it was puffy on the shoulder. She wore her hair long and straight with a part down the middle. Her walk was everything and her smile made me want to just forget about the code and approach her, but I chilled.

It was weird, usually, once any of my boys claim a girl, she's immediately unappealing to me, but I couldn't keep my eyes or thoughts off of *Stink, or Jhonni*e.

It was a good night. Pop Dean was a proud father that night, he kept saying his last was grown. He walked up and greeted us, he turned to Logan.

"So, where's this young lady I keep hearing about" Logan quickly left to get Stink.

Before he brought her over, Pop Dean looked at her strangely. I saw it but he played it off as he whispered something to Levi then walked off.

"Will you excuse us for a minute" Levi put his arm underneath mine and led me away from the ladies I was conversing with.

"Pops wanna speak to us" he walked off as Pop Dean announced over the mic needing all Murphy Boys, including me to the back.

We all gathered in a room, Pop Dean looked at us as we filed in, one after the other.

"Lo, where's this girl from" he asked with a serious face as he waited for the answer.

LeRoy being the big brother, the protector, stood up, "Yo Pop, what's going on" he stepped in front of Logan who was looking like a deer caught in headlights.

"I uh..." Pop Dean wiped his mouth as he turned to face us. "That girl MaJhonnie, I think she could be your sister" he said looking at the ground.

We all reacted very differently. Of course, we were all confused, but became doubly confused when Pop Dean asked her mother's name and Logan said, "Her Mom name is Celeste"

Pop looked at Logan questioningly, "And how old is she" he asked sitting down.

Logan thought, well she's older than me" he advised.

Levi interjected, "Yeah, she's a few months younger than me, she's cool. I talked to her; we know some of the same people" he said.

Pop shook his head. "So, she's 23, 24 no 23" he said, and they nodded.

He looked off in thought, "And she's from around here?" he asked.

Levi and Logan nodded. "Yeah, like fifteen minutes off the highway from here on this side of the bridge" Levi said.

Pop nodded, "Okay, well I gotta figure out some things and I'll get back with y'all. But in the meantime," he pointed at Logan. "Don't say or do anything to her, I mean it Lo" he warned.

Logan threw his hands up. "What type of man you think I am, I'm fucked up right now" Logan responded taking another shot.

We were in mid-toast, preparing to give well wishes, when we got notice that Jhonnie was about to shut down the party fighting with *Shamira,* Logan's self-proclaimed 'forever girlfriend'.

Levi shook his head, "Shamira has beaten up every girl Logan has tried to move on with" he said putting his drink down.

We all followed Logan back out into the party. Boy looked back at us, "Until now" he joked.

When we got to the front, Jhonnie had Shamira against the wall with her forearm to her neck, talking trash to her.

"Oh, she's definitely not what Shamira thought" Levi chimed in.

After separating the girls, we went back in the room, we all joked about the fight as we waited for Pops to give us his 'wrap up' orders. Pops walked out after telling us how much he loved us.

I thought about Stink and her fighting, she was one of the more proper cousins. But seeing Stink in action, she is definitely a chip off the old Demby block.

"Another toast fellas" Pudd proposed a toast.

We raised our glasses, "To Da Baby, welcome to it" we cheered for Logan as we drank our shots.

Logan walked out to get back to his party. "Catch y'all out there" he slid his glass across the table.

"How 'bout *that* shit" Levi said as he handed me a plate.

"I know Bop happy" I looked over at Pudd.

"Of course, I'm happy I'm here with my brothers" I replied.

Pudd laughed, "Uh huh, but be honest" he leaned closer. "You're happy as hell she might be our sister, well our sister, no blood to you. That mean she's fair game, now right?" he asked smiling.

I put my hand up. "Aye man, that's not my claim to fame" I sipped my drink.

I had to push down my curiosity of *Jhonnie*, maybe I wasn't carrying it as cool as I thought.

The possibility was intriguing, if she's a sister to them, then technically she's supposed to be like a sister to me. Only I don't want to be her brother, hell bad enough I was already fighting hard not to be her *cousin*. But that's a whole 'notha story.

Pudd was deep in my business reading my thoughts, "Honestly, if she is our sister" he glanced at Levi then sipped his drink. "I'd *prefer* her with you" Pudd said before biting his chicken.

"I agree" Levi raised his drink.

Pudd looked around then laughed. "Bop, if she is our sister, you have my blessing. Just know I'll shoot you if you do her wrong, just like I would anybody else for hurting one of my siblings, no questions asked. But for you Bop, I won't lay you cross the dirt" he sat back wiping his hands.

Pudd jumped up and jogged around the table to me. "Matter fact, just because it's you" he scanned me from head to toe. "I'll just shoot you in ya pinky toe on some Harlem nights shit" he joked as he fell into me.

We all laughed about that movie., and even though we laughed, I heard them loud and clear. I know one thing about this family...they don't play games when it comes to protecting each other, especially them damn Murphy Brother's...

I was on my way home when my phone chimed. It was one of my closest friend's next to Lo and his family. "Yooo" I said into the phone.

"Where you at come through, we on the block" I agreed and ended the call.

I did a U turn across Market Ave and headed back towards the block. The block was packed when I turned the corner. I double parked and threw my hazard lights on. It was a lot of commotion for this time of morning, but it wasn't surprising.

However, the scene I saw when I walked through the crowd was very surprising. Stink was laying on her horn then yelled for everybody to shut up.

"I need one of y'all to come put the car in park, if I move, my car is gon' move and I don't wanna hit no goddam body" she yelled.

Fetta was backing everybody away from the car. "We gon let em rumble" he looked over at me. "Rash, put the car in park for Stink" he ordered.

Jhonnie's girl cousins were standing at attention behind Quran, Jhonnie's youngest uncle. I leaned inside and slid the gear to park.

"Rhyon, open the door" she leaned on the horn again then yelled.

I could not believe what I was seeing but, I watched Jhonnie hold Shamira against the window by her hair and her arm. It was pure comedy to hear Jhonnie talk trash to her as she would occasionally bang her head into the window.

"Stink, let her go so I can open the door" Fetta pleaded with her.

"Ey Rhy-on, open the fucking door" she yelled.

"Stink, if I open the door with you holding her like that..." he tried to explain.

Jhonnie cut her eyes over her shoulder at me. "Rash, just pop the handle please, I just need the door unlatched" she explained.

I reached my arm over and pulled the handle towards me. Jhonnie hopped out the car still holding Shamira by her hair and arm through the window with one hand.

"Now, whatchu was saying? Remember when I said lemme park? Huh?" Jhonnie asked as she punched Shamira in her side.

"Oh shit" was all I could say as one of Shamira's friends flinched and "da girl cousins" mopped the street with them.

The insane thing is they fought it out and we were able to de-escalate everything and not one siren was heard.

"The neighbors on this block know if you see it popping; you, betta enjoy the show! You bet not call no goddam cops" Fetta said as we walked into his mom house.

"So, what the fuck happened, which one of them damn Murphy's sent that girl for my lil cousin?" he asked.

I held my hands up to object, "Hell naw, it's not like that" I started to explain.

"And one of them grabbed her?" he asked.

"I mean only to get her off ole girl's ass but that's it" I explained the situation.

"Stink, that's how it went down? You cool" Fetta asked looking at her.

"Yeah Rhyon, I'm good" he kissed her forehead and walked away.

"What the fuck is going on? Fetta don't know you're fuckin with Lo and that was his ex?" I whispered at her.

Jhonnie shook her head, "Hell no, are you high?" she replied.

"Rhyon likes no one, his ideal guy for me...damn sure ain't Logan Murphy" she said looking into her purse.

"Put ya number in my phone" she handed me her phone.

"Ummm, what's your number, I don't know mine" she snatched my phone and dialed her number.

"Since you're so *deeply* rooted behind my back, stay connected in my face" she walked away but looked back. "So why can't I call you Rash around them again?" she asked.

I rubbed my beard, "Because some folks don't know me as Rash. I'm Bop from Up Top back home and that's how I'd like it to stay" I raised my eyebrows and shrugged.

"Well, that's gonna be hard, I met you as Rasheed, you've been Rash all this time! Now I gotta call you Bop?" she inquired.

"Listen, I just found out your name was MaJhonnie *this year,* if you don't skidaddle" I said walking away.

"See you around Bop" she called out.

I hoped so, I just wished I was as prepared when that time came around.

Chapter 12: Jhonnie

"Best of Both World's..."

So, let me back up and fill you in on the time Rasheed "Bop" Oliver introduced himself into my life. He says we met years before, but this is when I finally started to pay him any attention.

My cousin Rhyon had purchased a foreclosed property. One that had started being built and then construction stopped. Well, him and his friends finished it and he moved in and had everyone over for a party before he furnished it.

A few of the girl cousins came to the housewarming, Brandi just had to announce my ignorance of Rasheed, so my cousin Missy chimes in "Stink, you really don't remember Rash, growing up, he was always at my mom's house with my brother. You've met him before!" she exclaimed at my inability to recall ever meeting him.

"Yall know I don't usually pay their friends any mind, who did he used to mess with? He ain't mess with any of *the girl cousins, right*? Please say no!" I inquired and everyone drew a blank.

"I don't think I've ever seen Rash with any *one* girl, in all the years I've known him" Brandi shared.

"Yeah, and you already know can't none of us mess with him, ole Sir Brother Fetta hatin' ass because lord knows ole Rash can get it" Missy said as she looked at him over her glass.

Rasheed definitely had my interest and judging by these seductive looks and smirks he keeps giving me, I have his as well.

Of course, he flirted but nothing ever came from it.

Fast forward to a few years later, I was over Rafiq's house standing in the shower growing irritated at whichever chick knocking at his door ended him 'making it up to me' in the shower.

I turned off the water and noticed my phone was ringing. It was my cousin Brandi. "What time you coming to the house?" she asked not even saying hello.

"Where are you? You sound like you're mobile?" I asked.

"Girl" she sighed.

I already knew this was gonna be a story, "Oh boy" I replied.

"Right, all of that on this blessed day of the Lord" she said, and we laughed.

"So, I spent the night out and now Terrence is blowing my phone up. Child, I lied and said I was up early running errands so I'm on my way home after I get some milk from the store because he's there waiting" she said laughing.

"Perfect, come get me, girl I gotta get outta here" I whispered.

"Huh? What the hell, I thought you was coming later" she replied

"Don't worry 'bout what the fuck I be doin', just come get me" I ended the call.

Now during the conversation, I done tip-toed into the hallway to hear Rafiq going back and forth with yet another girl.

Before I *kirk da fuck out* in Fiki's place, I just agreed, it's time to go. His quick cooperation with me leaving was proof that I heard what I thought I heard...he asked her for an hour to *tie up loose ends*.

Oh yea? Loose end? I got ya loose end...of course I let him know that I heard him,

You might wanna wash ya face! Hurry up now, you only have an hour..." I snatched the door by the handle out of his hand.

I barely closed the door before she started her fussing, "Girl, what the hell" my cousin Brandi said as she pulls away from Rafiq's house.

"Drama! Yes, child on this *blessed day of the Lord*" I said leaning into the seat.

Brandi points at her ringing phone. "I'm so glad you called because *guess who's in town?"* she said before answering her phone.

"Hey Rhyon" she perked up in her seat.

"Where y'all at? We at ya house" he said.

"Whatchu doin' here? I thought you weren't coming, I had to run out" she said.

"Well, I'm here so bring ya ass! Oh, and who's this scary guy parked in front of your house?" Rhyon asked.

"Oh boy, leave him alone, we coming" I said then pressed the button to end the call.

"Girl, so you know you're gonna have to leave ya bag in the car, he's so nosy. He's been calling since the sun came up being the *daddy-brother*. You already know he is asking 'bout you and your phone going to voicemail" she shared.

I rolled my eyes not even in the mood for it, we pulled into her driveway next to his car. I was not feeling it until I heard my cousin greet someone as she got out of the car.

"Hey Rash" Brandi said waving then hugging a tall, formerly chubby, now super sexy dude with a beard and a perfect smile.

I followed Brandi into the house and into her room, "Oh-kay, who the hell is that?" I pointed behind me.

Brandi laughed, "You know Rasheed! Come on Stink, we've been through this...ok I really think you should stop smoking. Him and Rhyon been friends for years" she sighed.

I cut her off, "Shut the hell up, I know that's Rash ok but the Rasheed I remember didn't look like that so...what the fuck? Where's he been? And girl he doesn't have to look that damn good" I said whispering moving further into her room.

She started laughing, "Oh my bad! But yeah girl, he just moved back in the states like a year or so ago, he played ball in Germany" she shared.

"So, he's friends with Rhyon and he ain't never mess with a girl cousin?" I said plotting.

I didn't really care about who he was with now...I was just relieved to know we weren't related, and he was fair game.

The housewarming was nice, Brandi's co-workers seemed pleasant. Of course, Rhyon had piqued two of the young ladies interest.

"It's nice seeing you again Stink" I heard from over my shoulder.

I turned around to see Rasheed standing behind me putting his hoodie over his head. He smiled and I smiled back at him.

The party had ended for her work friends and elders. Fetta invited a few friends over and Brandi invited a few of her friends, and it quickly turned into a "kick it". I knew once someone pulled out a deck of cards, there went the rest of my night.

I slid into a seat, ready to talk shit when I looked over at Rasheed as he sat in the seat across from me. He rubbed his head, smoothed his beard then hit me with the LL Cool J.

"First hand bids itself, right? I gotchu Stink, let's go" he said then tapped the table after picking up the cards.

What can I say, we ran everybody off the table. He let me talk shit and backed me up when I jumped out there and almost tanked us. We had a nice vibe.

He had his phone hooked up to Brandi's speakers, he played DJ after Rhyon kicked her off duty but then he went for a ride with ole girl, so Rasheed saved the party.

He played a series of songs to get my attention, definitely mood setting music with the occasional sexy glance following a subtle innuendo that was in a song lyric.

Oh, he's really flirting with me...

I finally gave up my seat to get something to eat. Rasheed didn't want to play with anyone else, so he got up from the table as well.

He followed me into the kitchen, "Hey listen, how exactly are you related to Fetta?" he asked me.

I took the plate from his hand, "My dad and his mother were siblings" I said piling food onto my plate.

"Oh ok, you're Uncle Stuy's daughter, right ok..." he said then quickly made mention that meant we weren't blood related, *which was a good thing*.

"No but I hear you're like family" I said sitting at the table to eat.

"You know how that whole, *my mom's best friend is my aunt* thing goes. Me and Fetta started hanging and I became a nephew and a cousin" he explained.

He looked at me as if to say, 'But I'm not tryna be your cousin though!'

"Send me that playlist" I asked wanting to hear a few songs he played earlier that evening.

We chatted for the rest of the night, we exchanged numbers and even engaged in conversation in the following weeks via telephone and video chat.

Then I changed my number and didn't see Rasheed again until I met him as Bop. Bop, being the best friend to Logan Murphy aka the guy I met on a plane that turned out to be my brother.

Rash was able to grab my attention for a while after the results, during one of the times my brothers *'put Fiki on knockoff',* which meant no communication.

The first time happened after Rafiq popped in town and they insisted I bring him to my Dad's for dinner, only for them to have a bunch of secret meetings and weird looks all night. I mean it was so uncomfortable, I gladly accepted Sofiya's ride to leave.

Sofiya advised me that she was leaving the country for a few weeks and wanted to give me a few things, so I agreed to come spend time at her hotel but, I had plans later.

Shit! Now, I had to find a way to get away because you heard me when I said, Rafiq popped into town. My favorite brother agreed to be my alibi.

This is how it works; they'll give me a time to call their phone, they'd ignore the first call and then I'd call back two more times; on the third time they'd answer, and I'd say, "I need you to come get me" in a panic then it's up to them to get out of whatever they're in.

Well, tonight, I chose Levi because out of all of them, he only uses me to just get away from ole girl. He doesn't ask questions like them other two, he understands, you might just need a break.

I jumped in my car and drove across the bridge then hit the highway. I pulled onto his block and quickly spotted his car; it was parked on the street. I thought for a minute then pulled into his driveway. I pressed his name, "I'm out here, you want me to pull in?" I asked.

He ended the call and his garage door opened, "Yeah, he's with the shits" I thought as I pulled inside.

A few minutes later, the garage door closed, and he opened another door, and a light came on. He walked down to my car and opened the door.

"Whassup Stink" he opened my backdoor to grab my bag.

I got out of the car and stood in front of him, "Hey Rash" I said sliding my arms around his waist and leaning into his embrace.

Rasheed's body was solid but soft and I loved to squeeze on him. He put his arm around my shoulder and pulled me close, "Took you long enough" he said moving over to let me walk into the house first.

"My bad, had a few surprises, mishaps and tragedies today" I said lightly.

He chuckled, "Yeah, I heard, but where you going? Come 'ere" he said pulling me back.

Rasheed put my arms around his neck, he bent down and wrapped his arms around my waist then lifted me onto the half wall separating his dining area. He put his hands on my thighs then rested his face into my neck and just inhaled me.

"Damn, I've been waiting for this" he said with his nose pressed against my neck.

"Oh yea, you missed me?" I asked.

"I told you I missed you! So much so I went straight to Pudd's from the airport hoping I saw you" he kissed my nose.

I leaned back and looked at him. He smoothed my bun then stood up, "So when was you gon tell me about ya outta town visitor?" he raised his eyebrow at me.

"Umm..." I rubbed my eyes as I tried to think of how to explain Rafiq and his unwanted pop-up.

"Let me stop you, before you get all into y'all history, I really only have one question" he stepped closer to me.

Rasheed smoothed my hair back then he touched my face, "Are you with him for real?" he asked.

And it seemed so simple, but I stuttered then I just gave up and let out a heavy sigh, "I don't know what we're doing" I shrugged giving him an honest answer.

I really didn't know...

"Well for us to have the night we talked about, you're gonna have to know" he demanded.

"Rafiq, he's hard to explain. We do have history, but I would never put him in your face like that, he popped up and the boys insisted that he come to dinner" I explained hoping he understood.

Rasheed took my hand and led me into a spare room. He had a massage table set up with candles lit and music playing. "I knew you had a stressful week, so I had planned to help you relax" he walked over and laid blankets on the table.

"May I" he lifted my arm and helped me remove my jacket.

Rasheed began removing my clothing as he asked about my day. I loved how he made me feel in this moment. I had never been undressed as intimately as Rasheed did that night. I stood in front of him with my hands to my side. He leaned down and kissed my forehead.

Rasheed moved the blanket, then helped me up onto the table. He positioned and adjusted my body on the table, then he covered me with a warm blanket. I opened my eyes and looked up at him.

"Close your eyes" was the last thing I recalled before I felt him remove the blanket from my arms and he massaged and rubbed my neck and shoulders before moving to my arms.

That shit was amazing, the smell of the oil filled the room. I inhaled as he rubbed up my body then let it out slow as he rubbed down my body.

It felt so good that I stopped counting but I woke myself up at least three times from the sound of my own snore. Rasheed gave me a full body massage with everything but a happy ending.

Rasheed brought my bag into the guestroom and then stood by the door. "Because I'm a man of my word, you got your massage but, I keep telling you and you don't seem to get it. *I don't share"* he said, and he backed out of the room.

"You already know how I feel about you out this time of night, you're welcome to stay here until the morning, or I'll drive you back to your hotel" he offered.

"Rash, are you forreal?" I asked walking over in front of him. I wrapped the blanket and looked at him.

"I thought we agreed not to ask any questions, I don't care about who you're with when I'm not around?" I fired back at him knowing there had to be someone, but I clearly didn't care.

I unwrapped the blanket and let it drop to my feet, "You really gon rub all on me and then send me home?" I asked putting his hands on my hips.

Rasheed groaned and closed his eyes, "Whatchu want me to beg" I said leaning in so close to him, that our lips touched.

Rasheed looked at me and smirked, "Fuck it" he started kissing me as he backed me onto the bed.

I'm pulling his shirt off, he is sucking on my breasts, we're rubbing and hugging and getting down to it. He flips me over and smacks my ass, then bites my cheek.

Bom...bom...bom...bom...bom...

We both jumped at someone doing a cop knock on his door. I looked at the dresser, the clock read 1:45am.

He looked at me as he walked down the hallway then backed up to the room.

"It's your brothers" he said closing the door.

The boys came in loud like it wasn't almost two in the morning. I hurried up and got dressed as Rash came into the room. "Come over into my room and chill until your brothers leave" he said carrying my bag across the hall.

"Hurry up" he waved me across the hall.

He had just closed the door when Levi came upstairs asking for something.

I stood with my back to the door and held my breath as Rasheed hurried up out of the room to stop him from coming all the way to his door.

"I gotchu, it's in the basement" he said as they walked down the hallway.

I tried to listen to them talking but I couldn't hear everything, so it just frustrated me. I turned on his television and climbed into his bed. I pulled the blanket over my shoulders and quickly fell asleep.

I opened my eyes when I felt someone kissing my face. "Stink, guess what? We got problems" he said kissing my face and down my arms.

"What's wrong?" I asked rolling over and pulling the blanket closer.

"Ya brothers are downstairs sleep, they're talking 'bout staying here until it's time to go handle business" he shared.

My eyes opened and I sat up to look at him, "What does that mean" I whispered.

"Unless you want them to know, you gon have to chill a little longer than expected" he shared making his eyebrows dance.

He abruptly got up and left the room, then I heard Logan in the hallway. I hurried up and ducked under his plush comforters. I ruffled the oversized comforter to try and hide me in the bed.

"Yo Bop, I still got a hoodie and boots here?" he asked loudly having no concept of time.

It's five in the gotdamn morning, why is he wide awake?

"Yeah, I'll get it" Bop said in a rushed response.

"Whoa, hold up" he said before walking into the room, he stopped Logan from coming in after him.

"Oh, my bad, whatchu entertaining? Why you ain't say something? Dayyuummn...my bad" Logan said lowering his voice.

I heard Logan go downstairs, I waited until I heard Rasheed call my name a second time. My ruffling of the comforter worked, even he couldn't see me, and he knew I was here.

"Stink" he said ripping my blanket off of me. "You're funny" he said laughing at me curled up on the bed.

"Shut up!" I snatched the blanket from him.

"How did you know he was coming" I asked settling back into the bed.

"He always hits the light at the top of the hallway, it's like a jump shot if he runs upstairs" he explained.

"See if you woulda let me get that *or let me leave; we wouldn't have these problems"* I muttered as I slid against his sheets trying to get comfortable.

He waited until I was finished moving and *shit talkin'* before he leaned on the bed. I immediately got nervous because he said, "*What I tell you bout that? Let you get that?*" he asked while grabbing my ankle and pulling me across the bed.

"Nah, we woulda been caught because ya brother got a key to my place" he shared.

He knelt on the bed and wrapped my legs around his waist. "You're not ready, so stop talking shit because you know I respect you too much to trash you with ya family downstairs because how I'm feeling looking at you in my bed right now" he paused then took my hand to make sure I felt him in all of his manhood.

"I'm ready to let you get that" he said as his deep voice vibrated my bottom parts.

I waaannntttt itttttt!!!!!! I screamed to myself as I took in all of his masculine alpha male energy. The light from the television let me see him smiling at me as he massaged himself and rubbed my leg while he held it against his chest.

"Can I kiss you?" he asked.

I nodded my head, I tried to open my mouth to respond but only a soft moan escaped my lips as he kissed the back of my knee then leaned down and kissed my chin, then my cheek, my forehead, my hand and then he took both hands and held them over my head.

He kissed my cheek again, "I gotta go, but I hope you're still here when I get back" he said looking into my eyes. "I wanna *really kiss you..."* he said biting his bottom lip.

"And I really wanna be kissed" I said back to him.

Rasheed smiled as he leaned down and gave me the softest, deepest, stomach dropping kiss as he applied pressure to my wrists as I tried to move. By this time into the kiss, I'm grinding against him just trying to feel him again, h*e's got some weight on him, but he's just teasing me.* Rasheed kept moving.

He taps my hips as he kisses my lips again then pushed off the bed. "If you gotta go, I'll understand just use this" he put a remote to operate his garage door on the nightstand.

"You want me to meet you later for it?" I asked.

"Guess that means you won't be here when I get back" he said pulling his hoodie over his head then grabbing Logan's stuff out of his closet.

"Not that I don't want to be, I have to take Sofiya and him to the airport, I gotta run some errands then hooking up with the girl cousins" I explained my day to him.

"Then hold onto it and use it when you come back tonight after ya hangout, I want to see you before I leave" he kissed my lips again and walked out.

I sat in bed laughing as I listened to them be such boys cracking jokes about how *Bop had company.*

They kept making comments and even apologized to me for *taking him away but promised to bring him back soon so we can finish.*

I typed a message to him, *'Do you think they'd be clowning if they knew it was me?'*

'Abso-fucking-lutely not, and they all here even a few of ya cousins' he replied.

"I ain't tryna die for it" he sent back.

I dropped my phone in my bag as I headed to the bathroom. A few seconds later my phone started ringing.

SHIITT!!! I scrambled to my bag and forget about silencing my ringing phone, I powered that bitch off. I knew from the screen it was Levi. I hope he didn't match up the rings.

It took them a minute, but they finally left the house, I waited until I heard multiple car doors close, and ignitions start before I moved from the squatted position I was in on the floor on the side of his bed, next to my bag. I slowly stood up and saw Rasheed's truck pull away.

I powered my phone on and messages came through from Levi, my momma, and Rafiq...*dayuuumm*.

I opened his message, "I'm out here so tighten up, can't be with me no more" he said.

That is why I loved him! Levi was my favorite...easy!

I walked into his bathroom and turned on his shower, and that thing was phenomenal. He has six shower settings and shower fixtures in the walls with heated floors when you come out the shower.

Oh honey, Rasheed had a beautiful four-story townhouse that he and some friend's gutted and customized for him. The boy had style.

I walked into the room and looked at the remote on his nightstand. Well, let's see where this goes...

Sweet thangs, it goes bad, real fast! Turns out my Murphy family ain't Team Fiki, it wasn't my problem because if nothing else Fiki and I are friends, like since we were young, even if this doesn't last, we're still always friends.

Plus, no one wanted to give me any information as to what exactly their issue was so against my brother's directives that I *shouldn't* entertain Rafiq...I did and almost got caught up in some shit.

I was trying to have both Rasheed and Rafiq, being with them was like the best of both world's; mostly because Rasheed and I weren't sexually committed to each other.

It wasn't my fault, he wouldn't give me none, but he still courted me. So, I got double trips, gifts, and attention but only had to put out once. I was winning, or so I thought.

I should have known with my luck this good time was coming to an end. I was having too much damn fun. My worlds were starting to run parallel and even overlap at times.

It started with work, I was so deep in my bag of shit living the best of both world's that I forgot I was at work one day and this lady tried me while I was in Stink mode after hanging up a phone call.

Let's just say it didn't end well for her. She muttered something indirectly in my direction as she walked past into the copy room.

I caught her ass by the copier, "Janesta, I know you don't know me too well, and Darcy is your girl but" I said in an attempt to try and squash whatever beef she had with me.

Janesta cut me off, "You're right Jhonnie, she is my girl and that little stunt you pulled at the facility was childish and you really need to grow up" her face was screwed up as she spat her venomous filled words at me.

I could just imagine what's said about me when I'm not here. I had been ignoring the snide comments from the corny crew, but it seems like the quieter I was, the larger the group grew.

Terrence and I joked they were recruiting member for the "We hate Jhonnie" club. I had found ways of ignoring them in the past but *when the corny girl that the other corny girls think is corny tried me,* I had enough.

I looked over her shoulder and saw Terrence walk in and out of the bathroom. I nodded my head and he reached over and pulled the copier room door closed as he walked by.

And that's when I let her know, "Janesta, I don't know who you think you're talking too but don't make me come down Smuckers Road one Friday night and beat you the fuck up, it can happen. The only reason I don't drag you and ya corny crew is because I have way too much to lose, but please don't think I don't know a few *ain't shit bitches* that'll dog walk ya ass now..." I backed up as I walked over towards the door.

"I suggest you mind the business that pays you..." I said walking out of the room.

I had just returned from lunch to a message to report to HR. I was pulling out of the parking lot of my job when my cousins called me.

"These hoes so tough but ran to HR??" I yelled answering the phone.

"So, what did they say?" Missy and Brandi said into the screen.

"The bitch snitched, it's cool! Leemy just waiting to jump on her ass, but Ima chill for now. I took their paid time of reflection leave, which they only offered *because my work was done for the week,* and it's only Tuesday.

"The HR lady was cool; she knows Ant Dell. She was like, 'Demby? Do you know Delphine?' Once I said, 'Yes ma'am that's my Daddy's sister she was cool as hell" I replied making them laugh.

"I know that's right...Come through Ant Dell with the connections" Missy said.

"Naw she was like they give you three days leave while they investigate so they'd have an answer like next week" I explained the process as I understood it.

"So whatchu bouta do?" Brandi asked moving around her house.

"I'm coming to see you" I said to Brandi.

She blew raspberries, "Bitch bye, you not coming to see me! I'm going out of town with my Boo so sorry you gon have to find another alibi" she said laughing.

"I mean, you can stay here if you need too but you just can't be like *'oh me and Brandi did a thing'* because I'm bout to be low after tomorrow, matta fact if I call y'all like 'Aren't we going...just roll with it" she shared.

Me and Missy agreed, and we ended the call.

I hung up with my cousins and decided to go see my Mi-Mi. Imagine my surprise when I walked in and saw Rasheed. Now I hadn't seen Rasheed since that night at his house, we've chatted on the phone a few times.

He was in the kitchen, we made small talk and it took everything in me not to make him *gimme that* in one of these rooms in my Mi-Mi's house.

Rasheed at first glance makes you look twice. I've seen him in some of everything; sweats, jeans and hoodies, t shirts, cargos, suits and even seen him down to his good ole boxer briefs. His body looks great in whatever.

Today he had on a blue hoodie with khaki cargos and boots. He had his hat tucked behind him in his pants by the brim. He was fresh from the barbershop; you could see the outline from his razor-sharp cut.

"Where you coming from?" I asked him.

He looked up at me and smirked. "Running, just got a cut; 'bouta go home and get dressed. Where you going?" he asked sucking his fingers after he threw a few chips into his mouth.

"Excuse me, Ey Mi-Mi my bad whatchu wanted on ya sandwich? I was so hungry, I just started eating but I gotchu" he chuckled as he engaged in conversation with her.

His words were simple but his tone and the way he looked when he joked with my grandmother, made me blush. He was a real gentleman.

Rasheed came back into the kitchen to wash his hands before he started pulling out skillets and cutting boards. I sat back in observation, "What kinda sandwich..." I mumbled as I watched him go into the refrigerator for ingredients.

I was so mad he had to leave so he wasn't able to make me a sandwich. Mi-Mi was hating and wasn't trying to hear about us sharing.

"It's cool Mi, enjoy ya fancy sandwich" I kissed her cheek.

Rasheed walked me outside, "I ain't know you was back" I said opening my door.

He closed my door then leaned against it, "I'm not, I'm just here tying up loose ends I'm selling my place" he said.

I opened my glove box and picked up his garage remote. "Guess I won't be needing this" I handed it to him.

"Oh shit, I forgot you had this! But naw, I'm keeping that spot. I'm selling my condo" he smiled.

"Well give that back then" I said putting my hand out for the remote.

This is when I should have known he was not playing with me...

Rasheed unlocked and opened my door, he leaned in and put his hand behind my head and pulled me into a nasty, coochy stirring kinda kiss. He kissed my lips as he backed out and closed the door.

"How about after ya trip down South, and you iron out ya issues then come back and see me and I'll give you the keys" he said as he touched my face, "That's a bet?" he asked walking away.

I sat there watching his bowlegged self, walk over to his truck. I wanted him and that kiss didn't help my situation. He actually made it worse.

I have more important questions like, *how does he know I'm going South?*

"Love you Mi! I'll be back" he yelled, and her sarcastic response let me know she saw our show.

"Jhon-nie??" Mi-Mi called out my name from her porch.

I backed my car up to her view and rolled my passenger-side window down, "Yes ma'am" I replied smiling.

"Mmmm, I see you" she said as she waved and walked back into her house.

"Now what does that mean???

I looked over at Rasheed sitting in his truck signaling for me to roll my window down.

"I only came to get my grandmother's approval before I moved forward with my plan. Now that she gave her blessing, I'm not gon keep playing with you Stink, clean ya shit up" he said then pulled off.

I waited until he turned off the block, *then* I got out of the car and walked back into Mi-Mi's house.

I had walked inside to see Mi-Mi walking through the house towards the kitchen.

"Sit down" Mi-Mi pointed to a seat at the table. She placed a plate in front of me with half of her fancy sandwich on it. "You want some juice?" she asked.

I looked at the time as I moved around a few meetings. Clearly, we needed to talk, "Yes ma'am, um Mi-Mi... how does this work?" I asked.

"Bop just said, I just let my *grandmother* know so, is he really a grandy grand or not?" I asked.

Mi-Mi laughed, "Baby, it's not up to me *yet* to clear this up for you but until then let me put your precious mind to rest. Yes, Tatum is my grandy grand, but none of the children I birthed created him so you're good.

Mi-Mi sat across from me, "You know how close he is to your brothers, so you know how that goes but don't worry y'all not kissing cousins" she said letting me know she definitely saw that moment out front.

That didn't help...I was more confused and now uncomfortable. Rasheed is way, way, way too close to home.

Damn, I can't mess with him. I'm glad he took his remote back, now it's no reason to call. I gotta leave him alone.

Chapter 13: Levi

'This surely ain't what I thought...'

Jhonnie had finally agreed to a dunch, but she didn't want to talk to her mother. I tried to tell our Dad just to tell Celeste it was cancelled. He said he told her, the dinner was off, but she showed up anyway.

Jhonnie was already shaking when she arrived so I needed her to calm down before Celeste arrived.

I moved Jhonnie through the house, "Y'all seen Rebecca" I walked thru the house looking for Ram so she could help calm her friend. She has asthma and it's been triggering a lot lately but she has an inhaler so she should be cool, for now.

"I heard Jhonnie's here" Pop yelled out walking into the room.

"Yeah...but give her a minute Pop" I said holding my hand up.

I waved Ram over. "Ya girl in the guestroom off the kitchen, shaking like a stripper, go help her tighten up" I said pointing in the direction of the room.

Ram exclaimed, "Oh no! Okay let me go get her" she walked over to the stairs.

Boy and Pudd came over to me, "Where she at" they both inquired.

I asked them to give me some space, "Give me *and* her a minute" I sipped my drink before walking away.

Roy nodded his head then went back to his game of Dominoes.

Pudd announced food would be ready soon.

Celeste had arrived so that meant everyone was here, so we could begin.

Ram and MaJhonnie came out the room and they walked into the dining room; my Dad stood up to greet her. He hugged and kissed Jhonnie then introduced her to my grandmom and then the others.

Mi-Mi held Jhonnie's face in her hands and kissed her cheeks repeatedly then hugged her for what seemed like forever. Jhonnie and our aunt were the only females of age left in our family. There were four Murphy sisters and they all had sons except for Mi-Mi she has Denita, but she had all boys and her brothers had son's. We were s family of boys. There's seventeen of us, all boy cousins and now we have Jhonnie. She's the *Neet* of our generation.

So far so good dunch was going smoothly, until one of my cousins asked MaJhonnie's place in the family. Mi-Mi cleared her throat, "MaJhonnie is between Leviathan and Logan" and that's when they all caught on.

As he already admitted, our dad cheated on our mom. I mean we knew he wasn't the best husband based upon stories of his womanizing reputation but damn. Pop quickly changed the subject as Mi-Mi shushed the other chatter in the room.

"So Pop, you got starting five now huh" I said.

My pops laughed as he kissed Jhonnie's cheek, "Hell yeah, I got own Fab Five" he grinned then looked at us.

LeRoy, our eldest brother prayed over the food and we all enjoyed our meal and time together. Pudd was bringing desserts out when Logan stood up.

"Well since I made all this happen, I'll go first" Logan asked if someone could pass him the green bag off the counter.

"Wait, Lo actually put his gift in a bag" one of the cousins asked.

We clowned Logan for a bit because Logan never wraps presents, he says it's a waste.

"It is a waste, but I feel like this is a special occasion" he wiped his face as he turned to face MaJhonnie.

"So as yall know Jhonnie and I dated for a couple months, *before* I found out she was our sister! Thanks for the heads-up Pops" he joked.

Jhonnie sipped her drink and cut her eyes over to me. I could see her breathing was uneasy, so I moved to sit next to her. I took her hand and took deep breaths, she looked over at me and her slowed down her breathing.

We both went back to listening to Logan's story, "So Jhonnie since you *are* our sister, then it's only right that you sit at the table with your brothers. We got you some gifts to even the playing field from the siblings. *Anndd to show you* how happy we are to have you in our lives" he said smiling.

Logan handed Jhonnie the bag. "Let's give Jhonnie all her stuff first. I put ours in a green bag because that's her two of her favorite things. The color green and bags" he joked.

Jhonnie looked over at Ram who was standing behind me, then she looked at our hands still locked.

"Yea, the green bag is from me and Lo" I said as I put my arm around her, "We love you and whatever you need you already know you always got me" I said softly to her teary-eyed self.

"So, you always got us" all the brothers said in unison.

Jhonnie wiped a tear and hugged me back. She left her head on my shoulder as she listened to Roy present his gift.

"I was able to buy my lil *brothers* their first cars, and since you definitely don't need another car my gift to you is in equal value, so I gave you half of my rental property" Roy handed Jhonnie the deed to half of his duplex.

Lo jumped up, "Hell naw, where my property at" we laughed as Jhonnie quickly took the envelope and keys from Boy.

Boy looked at Logan, "It's parked in your driveway at the property we helped Pop get for you" Roy said.

Logan nodded his head, "You're right, my bad" Boy hugged Logan and he sat back down.

Logan and I both got Lexus cars from our older brothers when we turned eighteen. All the brothers shared a house until Pudd, and Boy helped Pops get us our own houses on our twenty first birthdays.

Pudd stood up and handed Jhonnie another envelope, "Pops always told us, our jobs as brothers is to share and make sure we take care of each other. Then I heard about *you* and then I met you. I thought what can I get a lady that already has a lot of shit?" Pudd looked around the room. "my bad Mi-Mi" he blew a kiss at her.

"I figure you can never have enough money so that's my gift. I gave you a share in my business. The others already got their return. Matta fact, there's another thang thang coming soon. But to my Lil One, here's your share of last year's profits" Pudd kissed Jhonnie on her cheek as she peeked into the envelope filled with large bills, including a few fifties.

Mi-Mi said what we were all thinking, "Oh my, Jhonnie *is* special, Pudd gave her cash" we joked and laughed about our brother's issue with giving up his actual money.

"Pudd is the richest, brok-est man I know. He never carries cash" Logan laughed.

Jhonnie put her envelope in her bag. "Well thank you Pudddd" she sang.

She blew a kiss, and he nodded his head. We all laughed as Jhonnie held her purse tightly in her lap.

Mi-Mi talked to Jhonnie about the importance of being the first girl in almost twenty-five years.

She gave Jhonnie a diamond tennis bracelet and said, "I have plenty more jewelry for you, since none of my boys will bring me a nice, respectable granddaughter, thank God, he gave me my very own" she finished.

We all objected. I raised my hand, "Mi-Mi" reminding her about Rebecca who was in fact in the room.

She waved her hands as she cackled, "I'm sorry Baby, yes Rebecca is still here and I'm so proud" everyone laughed, even I giggled at some of her comments of my past behaviors.

We hurried up and moved past that topic. Pop asked Jhonnie if she opened his box and she shook her head, "Uh yeah, about that...it's complicated" she offered with a funny shoulder shrugging, heading shake and a wave of her hand type gesture.

"In other words, not right now" she replied with a smile then quickly grabbed her glass.

Pop nodded and offered taking her out for dinner next week just the two of them. Jhonnie agreed before my Dad excused himself as Celeste began speaking to him. She followed him into the kitchen.

I could hear him trying to quiet her down, but she was not trying to hear it. He walked thru the dining room and into Pudd's office. Celeste was right on his heels as he hurried up and closed the door. And then it went down.

"I knew I shoulda never trusted yo ass" Celeste yelled as my father shushed her.

He told her to be patient, but she refused. "No, I want my bag and my money *now*, one of y'all betta find that bag" they went on with their argument.

"Why do you think one of us have it? And who else knows about this bag and ya money?" he asked growing annoyed I could tell by his tone.

I looked over to make sure Jhonnie wasn't in the room, but she was, I looked at her and she shook her head.

"I'm not surprised" Jhonnie said as she was typing into her phone.

Roy tried to turn music on to drown them out, but it's almost like Celeste wanted to be heard. Mi-Mi finally went to go shut them up.

A few minutes later, Celeste stormed through the dining room, "Let's go Jhonnie" she tried to grab her arm but Jhonnie moved out of her way.

"No, I'm staying. I don't know what exactly your deal in all of this *is* but I'm staying. It's a lot of mess going on, no I'm over it" she put her hand on her head.

Jhonnie looked at our Dad then at the rest of us as if to ask for help. We all looked at our father as Pudd was rocking from side to side. Everyone knew that meant he was counting, so we had to be ready.

"Celeste, she's good" Pop said with his hand stretched. "You can go, I'll call you" he said.

Celeste burned holes into him as she stared at him with fire in her eyes.

"Girl, if you don't git" Mi-Mi said as she stood up from her seat.

Celeste backed out of the room, then turned the corner to leave.

"Jhonnie let me talk to you for a minute" Pop said walking through the kitchen.

Once Jhonnie left the room, Pudd leaned into the dining room. "Baby girl was 'bout to be like Jazz, y'all was gon be calling me Uncle Phil" he gestured tossing Celeste out of the house.

"Naw, but on some real, how many times should someone have to ask you to leave before you do it?" LeRoy asked.

"I wanna know what money she's referring too" Logan said drinking his juice.

I pointed at my brother, "That's the question" I shook my head.

He extended his fist towards me. "My man" Logan said.

Jhonnie came back holding another envelope. "What I tell you, grown-ups ain't shit sometimes" she said holding it up. "I'm almost scared to open this shit" she said picking up her drink.

"Oops, my bad Mi-Mi" she blew a kiss after Mi-Mi cleared her throat a second time.

Pudd sat a plate in front of her with peach cobbler cake on it. "Here Sis, try that! It'll make you feel better" he kissed her cheek and walked away. Jhonnie began eating the cake, I leaned over and whispered to let her know it was a weed treat.

Jhonnie looked at me, "Yeah, I suggest you save the rest for when you're safely at home" I said laughing.

Jhonnie picked up the pitcher of cucumber and lemon water. "These are *mint leaves, right?*" she asked.

Rebecca laughed, "Yes, that's *my* water" Jhonnie nodded and poured herself a glass.

"Now I gotta get ready to go home before this shit hits me. What about the cookies? Those aren't treats too are they?" she asked looking at the crumbs on the empty tray that we ate off of all night.

"Lemme get ya coat! Lo get ready to get Jhonnie home! Sis bout to either tweek out or have a long winter's nap" I joked.

"Boy, I can drive myself" she fired back but when Logan sat down, she rescinded her independent attitude.

"Oh no, I still need you to help me to the car" she said putting her coat on.

Jhonnie did her rounds saying goodnight to the family. Later after the majority had left and it was the brothers and a few closer than the rest cousins, our dad explained that Celeste finally admitted that Jhonnie wasn't her daughter.

We don't know how he got her to admit that, but she shared she didn't care about any of *this* stuff she's just *'looking for a bag of money*.

I could tell Pops is playing with her, but we still had a million and five questions, we needed to know what the heck is going on, which he answered as best as he could. It had to be difficult for him to do, it was hard on us just hearing it.

Logan shook his head, "Ayo this is fucked up, like what else y'all gotta tell my sister, just tell her everything right now" he pointed at the ground.

"Y'all, not gon keep fuckin her up...*my bad"* his voice was shaky. "Ooo I'm getting hot just thinking 'bout it" he said rubbing his hands against his thighs and pouring water into his glass.

I nodded my head understanding his feelings of anger. Jhonnie's our sister now. It sits differently with us.

"Yeah, Jhonnie *has* been through a lot these past few years. She basically just found out her whole life has been a lie, all after she met *this* guy" I advised my brothers as much as I could without breaking her confidence.

"And let's not forget, she was just getting over her Dad's death. Only to find out, he wasn't her father *biologically and she's not an only child*" Rebecca added.

Logan reacted, "Awww man, we gotta do something for her. I feel bad as shit like dayyuummm and y'all see her? She is cool as hell with it. You would never know she's dealing with all this like, hell nah! Everybody gon know y'all fucked me over" he finished discussing how amazed at how Jhonnie could even sit in the room with Celeste.

"Oh no Jhonnie doesn't know that Celeste isn't her mom, that's a whole 'notha story" Pops said.

"Ima buy my sister that bag she wanted" he said with finality as he sat down.

Roy chimed in, "Look at what we just gave her like Jhonnie *should* know we fuck with her" he shared.

Logan jumped up in his seat, "Boy, if me, Lee and Pop wanna buy our sister the bag that she wants" he turned and looked at us.

"Yeah, I jumped out there! Fellas Ima need y'all help with this...that bag cost a couple dollars" he laughed putting his hood on.

"Dannngg" his voice cracked as he looked at the price again. "Nah but real shit, that was already owed to her. I want to do something for the shit we learned tonight" he explained.

We all agreed to get her another gift that weekend, which turned into me taking her out to get it because Pudd and Logan were going out of town.

"Damn, Pop" LeRoy said as he looked at our father with shared feelings of disappointment for all the bullshit.

Boy quickly brought us back to the point of how *fucked up this whole situation was and then our Dad shared it was deeper than Jhonnie.*
"I'll take that, I'll take all your looks and feelings. I'll take it because I don't regret a day of it. As a result of the short time, I had with Sofiya, you all are able to live the lives you've lived, she got me straight" he sipped his drink and chewed on the ice.

"Your mother's first time being locked-up, she was working with Sofiya's husband one night when he got arrested. A few weeks later, Sofiya approached me and..." he shrugged and sipped his drink.

"Oh wow, that kinda stuff never happens to me, chicks don't approach me on some 'get back' I'd be with it too Pops" Lo said shaking his hand.

"So, this Sofiya lady is Jhonnie's mom" LeRoy asked looking around the table.

Our father held up his finger as he walked out of the room. He came back with a wallet in his hand. He dug through the pockets and pulled out cards and sorted through them. He paused then dropped a picture on the table. I flipped the picture and looked at a lighter-skinned and smaller in stature version of Jhonnie.

"*This* is Sofiya" I held the picture up as I passed it to Logan.

Pudd snatched the picture and smiled, "Ms Fiyonna, I know her. Her and Ms Shug" he chuckled.

He showed us a picture of him and *Ms Fiyonna* on his phone. "One of my most faithful customers" he smiled.

Our father's face straightened. "Yeah, you know Sofiya alright" he chuckled. "I gave her prissy ass that name" Pop took the picture back from LeRoy.

"Well, there you go, call her Dad" Logan said as Pudd slid a piece of paper with Sofiya's name on it. We all hung out for another hour but when I saw Rebecca yawning, I decided to call it a night.

A few days later, Rebecca and I started talking about Jhonnie and Celeste on the way back to the house,

"So, let's say Sofiya is Jhonnie's moms, how did Celeste end up with her" I asked turning into traffic.

Rebecca shrugged just as clueless. "I don't know but ever since I've known Jhonnie, Celeste has been a mess" she yawned.

I changed the topic and started talking to Rebecca about the baby.

Oh yeah, I don't know if anyone shared the news but Rebecca's having my baby. We just told the family because she couldn't hide it after not partaking in festivities last week.

I looked over at her she was fast asleep snoring and all. Of course, once we got home, Rebecca was wide awake with a *taste for something*.

On cue, she opens the freezer and says, "I could really go for a popsicle" she sighed.

I stood waiting for her to come running because I had stopped at the store and picked up some during her mini nap in the car.

"Oh Babe, she leaned around the corner and smiled, "When did you get these" she held up a box of popsicles.

I looked over my shoulder at her as I was reading the mail. "When yo ass *wasn't* sleep" she cracked up laughing as she fell into my back and hugged me from behind.

We had a brief disagreement in the car after she woke up denying she had fallen asleep.

"Babe, I'm so sorry" she whined.

I pulled her close, "Listen, I get it! No, I don't get it, cut that shit out. If you fell asleep, you're sleep I'm not mad about that. I think we're past all that, so chill out! Ok?" I said looking at her.

She laid her head on my arm. "Yes, Leviathan" I took a deep breath. She knew I hated her saying my full name.

"What, Jhonnie gets to call you Leviathan and I can't? Isn't that your name?" she asked.

I snickered and started laughing. I turned around to pull her into a hug. I notice the more time I spend with my sister without her, the smarter the comments from my lady. She denies it but that shit is corny, she's my sister. It's like she's jealous and I don't like it!

"My baby don't never like to be wrong, it's okay I accept your apology, go head and finish loving me for saving your life with a popsicle" I said.

She pushed away from me, but then hugged me again, "You get on my nerves" she said.

I smacked her butt as she walked upstairs eating her popsicle in the winter.

I walked into the living room and turned on the television and went to sit down when I saw lights coming up the driveway.

"Ram, Lo and Pudd just pulled up" I yelled up the stairs.

"Oooo and don't eat my goodies from Pudd please, thank you" I heard her yell before she closed the door.

I walked to the front door to greet my brothers. "What's going on" Logan asked as he walked into the house.

"Shit, was in here watching TV, where y'all coming from " Logan sat in the big chair in the living room.

"Pudd had to drop off shit and he want me to take him to the airport tomorrow after we leave the spot so we're dropping my car off tonight" he shared grabbing for the remote.

Lo slid his phone over to me for me to see the text from our dad.

"My phone on the charger, it died while I was out" I said responding to Logan asking about my phone.
I looked at the message and nodded. "DNA test tomorrow huh" I smirked at my brothers.

"So, what y'all staying at ya crib again" I asked looking at Logan, he nodded his head.

"Yup, and Pudd said I can drive his ride while he's outta town" Logan announced.

I looked over at Pudd, he finally broke down and let Logan drive his coupe.

"You're going outta town again, you might as well move in with Lo, rent ya spot and save your money or Lo move with you and rent out his" I suggested.

Logan nodded his head, "Tell 'em again Lee!" Logan joked as he walked into the kitchen.

"Oh yeah, go get Becs stuff out the car" Logan said to Pudd as he threw him the keys.

After Logan walked into the kitchen, I looked at Pudd, "These visits outta town, business or pleasure" I asked.

Pudd jumped up, "You know me" he winked as he walked out to the car.

Pudd told me about this piece he had outta town that was pushing his goodies. "It's just something light Tuck" Pudd said after I confronted him about having his *things* in my place and some other things I had heard in the streets.

Lo came out the kitchen eating pasta, "Yo tell Becs this shit bangs" he sucked a noodle into his mouth giving a thumbs up.

"Really, you gotta do all that" I asked as he walked by and sat at the table.

"I'm hungry, Mi-Mi ain't cook tonight. Her and one of her friends went out for dinner and shit" Logan got up to get something to drink, "Ey Lee, yall got soda" I nodded as Pudd came back inside.

"Here's Becs cakes and shit" Pudd sat the boxes on the counter. I spun a box around and took out a cookie,

"So, what yall think about Sofiya?" I asked my brothers.

Logan fell back in his seat. "I thought she was dope as shit. I was hyped to go see her spot. I really wanted to like her" Logan said as he finished eating his food.

"Wait, what did I miss?" I asked picking up on Logan's usage of words in the past tense.

Pudd rolled up his smoke and lit it, "Yeah but I think it's more to that! That don't seem like her style" he explained.

"How 'bout when Mi-Mi said, 'Oh, you one of them Bradshaw's' and Ms. Fiyonna said, 'No Ma'am I am *thee one and only* Sofiya Bradshaw, please don't confuse me, I'm different" Pudd said smiling

Logan banged the table with his fist. "That's the part that made me want to like her because she had a lil spice with her shit" Logan said as he grabbed and slid the box of goodies over.

He pointed at it, "You put ya spin on these Pudd" he asked before taking a bite.

Pudd shook his head, "Naw, these for the shop" I answered for Pudd as I took the smoke from him.

Logan shrugged and grabbed a cookie and a cake pop, "Whatever, we blowing anyway right" Logan bit into the cookie as he took the smoke from me.
"I ate a Tupperware bowl full of these jawns earlier" Logan laughed. "On some fat boy shit watching Law and Order" he laughed.

"So, is anybody else feeling like Boy?" Pudd asked as he poured something to drink.

I shook my head, not really remembering my mom too much growing up. Logan and I were young when she died. I mean I loved my mom, but we didn't have what he and Pudd had, it wasn't the same for us.

"Y'all know Boy be in his feelings about mom" I said.

Logan shrugged, "Ion know why" he added.

Pudd shook his head, "We remember her before the drugs and prison and shit" he replied.

Logan nodded in agreement then bit into his cookie, "Yeah I guess" he said out loud.

"Ant Neet is who I look at as my mother. And as of this morning, Denita Elaine Murphy said she's straight, so I'm cool" he opened the box and picked up a brownie bite.

"I don't have a problem with Miss Fiyonna, I mean it's not like she's here tryna be our mom, *but* Jhonnie is our sister so if she's her mom? Then what?" Pudd inquired.

Lo took the smoke from Pudd, "If she's Jhonnie's mom then that means she means something to our Dad so it's no rap" he said.

"But then there's that hitch in this giddy-yup involving someone else in the family, this is what changed *everything, at least for me.* This is why I can't like her, she's the godmom or however it works to the guy that got Cam popped" Logan said totally catching me off guard.

"Yeah, you remember that shit when Cam was running with his Dad's side of his family and he got pulled over with them guns and drugs in his car...well supposedly Sofiya and her son pinned everything on Cam and by the time Ant Neet got there, he was already charged up" Logan explained.

"Wasn't you there when he was telling us this shit? No, you left!" Logan said.

Pudd began explaining how after I left, my Dad and Mi-Mi left, then Cameron, Ant Neeta's son, shared that he recognized Sofiya from the picture. "He said, he'll *never forget her"* Pudd said eating a cake pop.

Before long we had eaten too many of the cookies, pops and snack bars, there wasn't enough to go on the trays. Pudd made just enough for Jhonnie and Rams pop-up shop tomorrow.

"Jhonnie gon kill me" I said feeling the fear stirring in my gut.

I looked at Pudd actually feeling a little scared, "Pudd you gotta make some more" I turned to plead with my brother as I pulled out my wallet.

Logan shook his head, "We don't have time, stores are closed and we gotta be at the spot early" he rebutted playfully.

I started to get upset but quickly blew it off. "Don't worry 'bout it, I'll just get something in the morning from their favorite bakery" I said.

My brothers hugged me before leaving out.

I walked upstairs to climb in bed with Rebecca. I wrapped my arms around her as I pulled her closer to me, she leaned back against my chest.

I kissed her shoulder, "If I asked you to marry me, would you" I waited for her response.

Rebecca cleared her throat, 'Why because I'm pregnant, Babe we are good" she kissed my hand and told me to go to sleep. I closed my eyes and did just that, I quickly went off to my dreams.

The next morning, I woke up to Logan and Pudd ringing the bell. Rebecca was already downstairs. I heard the door open and close, then I heard Rebecca talking in that high pitched excited voice she uses when someone does something nice for her and she's impressed.

I slid my shirt over my head as I walked down the stairs to see Logan and Pudd standing in the kitchen waiting as Rebecca ate a cookie.

"Ooo and they're still warm" she danced holding her stomach as she hugged Logan, "I swear I don't care what they say about you Lo, you're my baby" she kissed his cheek again.

"What did he do?" I asked pouring myself some juice.

"He found an all-night grocery store so Pudd could make me some more goodies for the shop" Rebecca said gushing over him.

I looked at Logan impressed and grateful for him saving my ass. "Look at youuu, my man" I gave him a pound.

I walked to answer the door. "Yo sis, what it do?" I backed up and let Jhonnie walk in.

"Hi Tink, how are ya" Ram walked over and hugged Jhonnie. She hugged everyone then spotted the sticker on the box and she got excited.

"Ooo Pudd, you made em" she asked hugging Pudd as he nodded and kept talking on the phone.

Logan walked over and hugged Jhonnie, "Whatchu doing out these parts" he asked.

Jhonnie sat on the chair at the island. "Bout to ask Rebecca to take me to the airport after we finish set-up. I'm bout ski-daddle on up outta here for a bit" she said eating a piece of cake.

"You too, Pudd going to the airport too" I looked over at Jhonnie.

Jhonnie looked at Pudd, where you goin?" she asked.

Pudd shook his head as he put his phone in his pocket. "Never, would I ever tell *you* where I'm going" Pudd said making us all laugh.

Jhonnie sucked her teeth. "Well, my flight leaves at noon soo let's set it off on the left, shawty" I sang as I snapped my fingers.

Rebecca grabbed her keys, "Come on, let's go" she said waving bye to us.

Jhonnie handed her bag to Logan. He grabbed it out of her hand as he walked towards the door.

"I'll meet y'all at the spot, I gotta make a run first" Logan said before he walked out and closed the door.

I turned around to look at Pudd, "So you been up all-night baking huh" Pudd nodded his head as he typed on his phone.

He seemed distracted, "Lee, Ima leave my keys with you. Just in case you need to get to the basement storage spot for whatever" Pudd slid his keys across the countertop.

"Pudd, why the hell would I need to get in your spot" he shook his head and shrugged.

I thought about pushing the subject but decided against it, mostly because both of our phones started ringing.

Chapter 14: Jhonnie

'Damn, can I recover...'

After Levi left, I couldn't stop thinking about what he said, I can't believe that woman, it's always about money with her. I was so angry they had me in the room with *that* woman. *Ugghh, so irked and annoyed.*

I closed my eyes as the plane took off.

I had sent Rafiq a message, "Thank you, I needed this" I type.

Rafiq booked me a ticket. He offered to come to me, but I didn't need him coming to town, I had a lot of things *goings* on and even though I was still in my feelings when I learned he had a daughter; but after that disaster of a dunch. I needed time away. I quickly accepted his offer.

The day before my flight, Rafiq called to make sure I was still coming, he shared about going to the mall on the way home from the airport. As we were walking through, my phone started ringing. It was Rebecca. I sent a message asking was it important?

I know she was doing the pop-up shop, but I also know she's being nosy because Rafiq called me just as I was pulling up to leave.

Rebecca tried to be extra but thank God for Mr. Officer, with his flashing lights, she had to move on. I ignored her call again. But when she called again once we got back to Rafiq's car I answered. Rafiq leaned over and kissed my cheek as he took the bags to put in the trunk.

"Ummmm just friends right" Rebecca said sarcastically and I ignored her.

"He did that in case you were a dude, he be so *joe* sometimes" I said.

"So, listen, real quick..." Rebecca lowered her voice then looked around. "Your father called some lady after you left his house, they kept calling her Ms Fiyonna. The boys were talking about it again, last night" she paused then looked around.

"*Supposedly*, the streets is saying that's yo momma, so the mystery is, *how the hell Celeste getchu...a*nndd this line is no longer secure" she muttered.

Just then Mi-Mi leaned in the screen and blew kisses.

Rebecca looked at the screen, "I'll call you later" she ended the call.

I shook my head laughing at Rebecca trying to discretely give me information.

Rafiq got into the car and looked at me and I smiled back thinking, I definitely needed to take time and look through that bag.

While we were riding from the mall, I looked over at Rafiq, "I'm not really into judging folks so please don't judge me" I said holding my hands to my chest.

"No judgement, what's up?" Rafiq shook his head.

I looked out the window. "I usually don't smoke when I'm away, and I brought it this time, but I need to smoke like right now" I shared pointing.

Rafiq laughed as he hit the steering wheel.

"Say no more" he laughed as he pulled open the ashtray.

He had just what I needed, it smelled so good. My boobs started tingling and my nipples got hard as soon as he lit it. I quicky kicked my shoes off.

He pulled on it then handed it to me, "Ya Uncle Sammy and aunts don't know do they?" Rafiq asked me. I shook my head.

I pulled my leg up to sit Indian style and inhaled. We rode in silence for a couple rotations before Rafiq shook his head as he grabbed and rubbed on my thighs.

"Say word, fuckin Jhonnie smokin' shotgun in my ride" he chuckled as he passed it back over to me.

Rafiq got sexy, very quickly to me as he kept running his tongue over his teeth. He would smile then lick his lips.

'This boy is trying to seduce me' I lightly laughed to myself. "Wait until I tell Brandi about this on Sunday" she invited me to her girlfriend's brunch when I told her I was coming to town.

Chapter 15: Rafiq

'This was supposed to be nice getaway…'

I took the scenic route home to give us time to enjoy our vibe. I scrolled thru my playlist and found some Jill Scott; chicks love Jilly from Philly.

I like to listen to her when I smoke with a female. Ness put me on to her during one of our road trips and I've been rocking out ever since.

"Whatchu know about her" Jhonnie dropped her head forward as she rolled her neck in circles then rolled her shoulders back.

I heard my mom in my head, *'If you want her, you gon have to work to get her!'* She told me that after Jhonnie's last visit that almost ended badly.

I circled around my neighborhood and headed back to my house.

"Oh my god, it looks like a split-level! I love it" she sang out.

I smiled at her giddy self, just smiling and bouncing in her seat.

"The only ones in town" I said cutting off the ignition.

Jhonnie got out of the truck and walked to the back. "I got ya bags here go open the door, 6250" I said then started moving things around.

She looked at me then took two steps back, "Whoa security codes and thangs" she joked as she walked to the house.

I picked up her bag and grabbed my gym bag, "I gotta work out tomorrow" I said walking inside.

"Well, I'm here until Wednesday, let me get some good sleep tonight and I'm game for whatever tomorrow.

I nodded my head, "That's a bet, here Ima put your bag in the room" I said pointing upstairs.

I grabbed both her bags and carried them to the guestroom. I put them in my guestroom. We chilled on the couch after we ate and ended up falling asleep.

The next morning, we got up and hit the streets early. I took Jhonnie to see Ness, she wanted to get her hair done. I used that time to beat the blocks up since I planned to be low for the next few days.

I swung through and picked Jhonnie up then headed back home. I walked in first, then headed upstairs to check the house. I grabbed Jhonnie's bags from the mall and took them into the guestroom, I checked the bathroom to make sure it was cool.

Jhonnie came upstairs calling my name, "In here" I yelled from the bathroom.

"Oh, this is nice, who's room is this, I know this ain't for me" she said as I closed the bathroom door. "Not with all the shit talkin' you been doin', uhn uh" she said.

"I mean I figured you would be comfortable in here. I didn't want to assume just because you got dressed in my room" I said.

Jhonnie laughed, "Maybe you're right but I think we owe it to ourselves to see if we're even a good fit *before* we invest anymore time" she blinked her long lashes at me, instantly turning me on.

I sat on the bed next to her. "Whatchu saying?" I asked.

Jhonnie stood up and threw her leg over mine and climbed on top of me. She sat on my lap and wrapped her legs around me.

"Let's see how much you've learned since high school" she kissed my cheek and then my lips.

I gripped her butt and positioned her right on top of me. She lifted up and smiled as she felt me.

"Oh yea" she asked. She wrapped her arms around my neck and pulled me close.

I smelled her and began kissing her neck. She grinded against me as she moaned and held me tightly. I squeezed and smacked her ass as I kissed up her neck.

"You don't know how bad I want you" I said as I bit her neck.

She looked at me and licked my lips, "Lemme see" she kissed me again before taking off her shirt.

I flipped her around and as I hovered over top of her, I looked into her eyes, "I'm not trying to just fuck you Jhonnie" I held her hand, then kissed it.

She nodded her head. "Understood, but can you fuck me tonight and still love me tomorrow? I didn't come all this way for love; right now, I need relief" she said rubbing my thighs.

I kissed her lips, "Say no more" I replied kissing her cheek.

I tore Jhonnie's ass up in that room. I think I heard her tap out. We had a good workout in my guestroom.

"First time I even *sat* on this bed" I joked as I kissed her forehead and drifted to sleep.

I woke up in the middle of the night, Jhonnie wasn't in bed. I got up to see where she went. After grabbing another shirt because I couldn't find my *beater,* I went to find her in the house.

"Jhon, where you at Babe" I yelled at the top of the staircase.

She answered me from downstairs. I fixed my boxers as I walked downstairs. I walked into the kitchen to see Jhonnie opening and closing the cabinet doors looking for something.

"You don't have any tea bags" she asked pulling out another drawer.

"No, I don't drink tea just because. We can get you some in the morning. Come back to bed" I said waving her over.

Jhonnie dropped her spoon on the counter, then turned off the whistling tea pot.

"How do you not have one tea bag in this whole *fuckin'* house" she said slamming the drawer. "I'm sorry" she put her hand on her head.

"I been going through the stuff my father gave me and I need to smoke. My whole head hurt right now" she folded her arms on the counter and put her head down.

I walked over to my condiments drawer and sorted through the different packets and bags.

"Huhn, here goes some tea my Godmom left here, I knew it was old. Does tea go bad?" I asked.

I threw some tea bags on the counter, "You want some honey too" she smiled as she smelled her tea bag.

"I need this to get my life together, tea makes me feel better" she held up a lotion bottle and asked for scissors.

I was curious, I definitely had questions, but I waited because I wanted to see what she had going on.

"There's scissors right here" I pointed at the knife set behind her as I picked them up.

"Gotta soften the plastic" she said adjusting her glasses.

Jhonnie grabbed the scissors out of my hand. She put the lotion bottle in the microwave for ten seconds. She picked up a towel and held the bottle over the trash and began to cut it open.

A big clump of something fell out into the bag she had strategically placed over the trash. Jhonnie picked the glob up and laid it on the paper towel. As she began to wipe and unwrap the glob, I realized it was four pre-rolled blunts.

Jhonnie looked at me, "You said you wouldn't judge" she said reminding me of her previous request.

I closed my mouth as I walked over to the counter to get a closer look.

"Did you just smuggle weed thru the airport" I asked not quite sure how I felt about it.

She giggled as she transferred the blunts into a girly looking cigar resealable pack, "Gotta keep 'em fresh" she said smiling.

"You talk about me, but I got me a *smoker smoker* huh? Look at you" I said as I got something to drink out the fridge.

She picked up her el and her teacup, then turned to sit it on the table. "My older brother. The loose one, he got me a bunch of goodies like that" she laughed. "But naw, I had too, last time I came Uncle Junie and 'nem played me out" she explained her last sober visit.

She looked up from the table. "I'm no drinker and they had me taking shots all night and you know I like to fight when I drink so that visit ended badly" she laughed as she lit it and looked over at me.

Jhonnie kicked a chair out for me to sit down. "Don't you think it's time we talked?" she asked as she blew smoke in the air.

I knew this shit was gonna happen sooner or later. "What you wanna talk about" I took the el out her fingers and turned my chair to face her.

"I want to know the truth, well your version at least" she said folding her legs ready for the story.

I inhaled and raised an eyebrow. I let the smoke out thru my nose and slid my tongue over my teeth.

"Al'ight, it is what it is right? I'll tell you whatever you want to know *if* you answer one question for me?" I leaned back in the chair.

She looked at me as if she was studying me before she nodded her head. "Oh-kay, go head" she said slowly sitting up in her chair.

"After everything that went down with ya snake ass ex, why'd you go back?" I asked dragging on the blunt then handed it to her.

I noticed her eyes got wide and she blinked a few times then she finally looked away. "Damn" she chuckled. "I knew you were going to bring that up" she snatched the el and folded her legs back.

She looked sexy as hell in my wife beater and her panties, sitting in my kitchen getting right and drinking tea. She is everything I need right now. You just don't get no realer than Jhonnie!

She looked over at me, "Thank you by the way, for *that*" she smiled as put her feet in my lap.

"Even the stuff on the inside?" I quickly added.

I looked up at her realizing that she never figured out it was me that got the dumb ass dude to leave her alone.

"So, why'd you do it, what was in it for you" she asked.

For a second, her question knocked me off my square, but after hearing what I heard about her new life, I couldn't blame her for being skeptical of me.

"I couldn't protect you anymore, I was getting transferred so I sent word to 'hold all calls' and he listened" I said with a shrug.

I cleared my throat as I rubbed her foot between my hands. I pulled my chair closer to her.

'You remember that year when my Dad told me that no matter what happens, I'm supposed to always take care of you like how he takes care of my mom?" I shrugged then looked at her, "so I did" I explained.

Jhonnie smirked at me as she thought over what I said. "I love your parents, especially your Dad. I mean ya mom is cool, but ya *Dad;* he was so dope" she sipped more of her tea.

"Yeah, that was the visit we were about sixteen, maybe seventeen years old and we chilled hard before you left to go overseas" she recalled that memory.

I nodded my head. I interjected, "I remember, I was on you heavy. I had talked to your Uncle to see if it was cool to approach you and everything" I recalled staring off into my thoughts.

Jhonnie objected not remembering the time of me expressing my feelings for her. I told her the story of how she turned me down for prom, which she also didn't recall happening.

"That was our last real summer together. Fiki, I would have remembered that" Jhonnie said with a smile but I was serious.

"Yeah, I chilled with you, even *after* you turned me down for prom" I said causing her to jerk in her seat.

"Rafiq, shut up" she quickly fired back.

I threw my hands up in my defense. "What, I mean...you did" I exclaimed loudly.

Jhonnie broke out into this hard laugh. "Oh, my goodness, Rafiq when did you even ask me to go on your prom?" she asked obviously playing with me.

I had to look at her to see if she was being for real, "Ayo, we were in my room talking about the prom, so I asked you and you hit me with 'that'll be a hard no'" I said imitating her voice.

Jhonnie jumped into an upright position sitting on the edge of her seat and got in my face.

"Oh my God Rafiq! And what did you say that made me give you that 'hard no'" she stared at me then laughed as she slid back in the chair.

"Oh, now you don't remember" she mumbled as she blew smoke in the air.

She looked up at me and blinked her long eyelashes. That shit was sexy as hell but no! Hell no! She almost got me, but I had a point to prove. *Stay focused Ski!!*

"Maaannn, bottom line you told me *no* and then you went to the corny guy prom" I said flagging my hand at her.

She looked at me. "I sure did because he *asked* me, very nicely I might add. And even though I was *his* date to *his* prom, he asked *me* what I wanted to wear" she said emphasizing her point with a lot of neck movements.

I rolled my eyes to the sky as she continued with her point.

"Whatever, he was a gentleman. He didn't start a conversation talking about 'how his prom night was going to go *this way* because 'his date *was going* to look like this and *she betta* act like that" she re-enacted my words from that night.

"Yeah, and then after all of that you had the nerve to turn to me and say, 'How 'bout you? Wouldn't you like something like that" she threw her hands back in disgust. "Just terrible" she shook her head as she relit and puffed on her el.

I looked at Jhonnie seeing that whole conversation thru a different set of eyes.

"So, I kindly said, 'um that'll be a hard no for me' and that was how you left it" she flagged her hand.

Jhonnie paused then pointed at me with a glaring look. "Are you telling me, *that* was your invite? Nothing in you felt like, 'Lemme try another way because I really want Jhonnie to go or how bout try asking me again when we were alone?" she looked at me as she poured more water into her mug.

I sat there feeling dumb as hell for not thinking of that. I shook my head firing back, "Naw, I just kept that shit moving" I replied.

Jhonnie giggled, "Clearly, in your feelings" she laughed as she folded her legs underneath her.

"My bad though forreal" I said looking at her.

I quickly changed the subject. "But anyway, back to how much I was feeling you. My Godmom was the only one that took that shit seriously. I was tryna get my mind and body right. I lost like forty pounds, hit the weight room and got it going.

She was on me the whole time. My Godmom wanted me to learn two languages and start my own thing before I finished school. I was on a roll, but then got caught up while I was away and almost got locked up for some years behind that shit" I shook my head.

"Yeah, I remember that everybody was pissed with you" she said as she blew smoke in the air.

I scoffed, "I *know* but when my godmom came to see me, she hit me with, 'they could work with the charges because the drugs weren't mine, so I was good" I looked at her and she gave me this look.

"Wait" she shook her head, "What does she mean you're good? Meaning what exactly" Jhonnie asked

I shrugged trying to spin my way out of this conversation, but she was like a prosecutor with a line of questions. I fumbled like an unprepared receiver; I knew I fucked up when I started stuttering.

"What reason would your Godmom be cool with a gun but not drugs, they're both synonymously bad" it was a long story that I didn't have the energy to share.

"Speaking of your Godmom, did you ever figure out what sparked her sudden interest in me" she asked.

I shrugged my shoulders trying hard to not *spill the beans*. Jhonnie cut me a side-eye, "You know, did you tell her to be nice to me or something" she asked.

I shook my head. "I didn't tell her anything, in fact she told me something" as soon as it left my lips, I regretted it.

"Wait, what? What did she tell you?" she asked smiling as she walked over to turn the stove back on to reheat her water.

I shook my head and quickly adjusted. "That we would be together" I said trying to play it off and not tell her the real reason for my Godmom's interest.

Jhonnie's eyes grew wide. "No, she didn't" she replied.

I went to get my phone. I scrolled to our old messages and found the text. I came back and showed it to Jhonnie.

Her face was solid as she read then she looked up at me.

I sat down looking at my phone, "Babe, what's wrong?" I asked.

"How do you say her name" she asked.

I looked at my phone because I didn't understand why Jhonnie's eyes were welling. "Godmom Fiyonna" I said regularly as tears fell down her face.

I sat down looking at my phone, "Baaaabe, come on, what's wrong" I asked again.

Jhonnie looked at me. "So supposedly Celeste ain't my mother, this Fiyonna lady, *your Godmom* is my real mom" she said wiping her face.

"Who told you?" I asked.

Jhonnie's face was confused as tears dropped out her eyes. It felt like something hit me in my stomach. Jhonnie looked at me like I was crazy.

"What do *you* mean, who told me? What aren't *you* telling me?" she asked.

I grabbed her hands. "I just found out I promise" I stated.

She looked at me, "How long ago is *just"* she tightened her lips and folded her arms across her chest.

I could tell by her demeanor, she'd be furious if I told her the truth, but I didn't want to be added to list of the people that has lied to her about this. Especially, since I still had more to tell her about me.

"Since the last time you came to visit" I replied.

She covered her mouth and began to cry. I wrapped my arms around her and pulled her close to me. She sat on my lap, "I'm sorry, but she wanted to find a way to tell you, she wanted to be sure" I said holding her.

Jhonnie pushed away and ran up the stairs. I noticed the sun was coming up as Jhonnie ran back downstairs with a small manilla envelope in her hands. She held up an envelope with my Godmom's real name written on it.

There aren't too many *Sofiya's, not spelled like this.* I anxiously watched her as she opened the envelope. "I was going to wait to go through this and some other stuff from this bag my bio-dad gave me, but..." she dropped some of the contents onto the floor.

Jhonnie picked up some papers as she fell back against her chair and held up a single picture. If I didn't know any better, I would have sworn it was Jhonnie in the photograph.

"Why can I see me here, but I don't see me when I look at her?" she asked.

I looked at Jhonnie then back at the picture of Godmom. "I dunno, we'll call her later and figure this out" I offered as a resolution.

Jhonnie shook her head. "Nope, call her now, matta fact get her here! She comes any other time you call" she walked back upstairs, and I heard a door slam.

I picked up my phone and pressed the call button. It was five in the morning but Godmom answered on the second ring.

"Everything okay Fiki" I took a deep breath and rubbed my eyes.

"Hey Godmom, I know it's early and kinda last minute but um, how soon can you come to town" I could hear her shuffling around.

"Well, your mom is picking me up Friday I can come by once I get there" she said in her cheery voice.

I looked up the stairs at the sound of Jhonnie crying as she was yelling at someone, she must be on the phone.

"What is all of that noise?" Godmom asked.

I held up a picture to the screen. She tried to focus on it. "I can't see it Fiki just tell me what's going on" Godmom advised.

I pointed above me. "That *noise* is Jhonnie crying and cussing somebody out at five in the morning because she opened an envelope and saw *this* picture that she got from a man named Dean Murphy who claims to be her real father *and* he told her you're her real mother" I took a breath to give her a chance to respond.

Godmom looked to her side. "I'll call you when I get there, I'm on my way" she ended the call.

I picked up the contents off the floor and put them back in the envelope. I cleaned off the table and headed upstairs. I jumped in the shower to rinse off before I climbed in bed. I had just fell into a calm when Jhonnie came to get in bed with me.

"Can I ask you a question" I opened my eyes, "You're not really my brother or cousin or young uncle, are you?" she asked.

"Shut up and get in the bed" I laughed as I lifted the comforter.

She climbed in bed and I pulled her closer towards me. "Naw, we're legit, but you want to know the crazy part? All my life I heard stories from my parents and Godmom of how they planned since the womb for their children to be together. On some real shit, we all thought you died; so, picture me fucked up right now" I said as Jhonnie looked over her shoulder at me.

"Seeee, I can't! I just finished cussing Celeste aka *the woman formerly known as my mother*, I left messages on all her voicemails. This is some bullshit, a whole bunch of bullshit" she spat angrily.

I shook my head to her news, but I agreed with her, it is one thing to not be sure of who your father is but then to also have to question your mother *before* you can confirm your father? That is a bit too much for one person to handle. I pulled her closer and held her a little tighter.

"Well, once she gets with my moms, they'll get here later this evening" I explained. "Meanwhile, the suns up and I'm just going to bed" I joked.

She nodded her head, "Ok so remember all that talk about *putting me to sleep*" she smiled at me.

After covering myself, I moved down in the bed then slid inside of her and wrapped my hand around her neck. I grabbed her hips with my other hand and began to slowly stroke her until she started shaking.

I kissed her face as I stroked her into a body shivering, toe clenching, sheet grabbing orgasm. As I was walking into the bathroom to clean off, she crawled up towards the pillows.

She pulled the blanket up and quickly fell asleep.

Chapter 16: Sofiya

'Well, this is where we are...'

I couldn't believe it when my new connect/darling friend named Pudd from 'Da Ville said we *needed* to talk, that he was gonna tell me he found *My Miss Dottie*. *I sure* didn't expect to find Jhonnie again through a third party, I was pissed at that Mr. Murphy.

After it came out and Dean was radio silent, I swore my silence right back to him. I wondered why Dean didn't reach out for me before he approached Jhonnie. I spent the majority of the trip 'up top', sending word for Dean to 'call me ASAP'. I spent the last few moments of the trip gathering my thoughts.

I finally got through the terminals and reached baggage claim, I couldn't contain my smile as I came down the escalator and saw Dean standing there. He got word I was coming so he came and picked me up from the airport.

Tuh, he got nerve like we cool... He betta had...

I greeted him and advised we needed to talk. I wanted to see his official documentation. I must say, getting a chance to see him in private was an added bonus. Dean still does it for me, in every way.

However, I did not let him know that. I was grateful for the interruption, I almost slipped and ended up in bed with him so imagine my heart dropping when Fiki called me with his news.

I turned to Dean, "We just agreed that you were going to let me tell her about me" I said as I ended the phone call.

'What are you talking about? I just gave Jhonnie the bag, but we haven't even spoken about it. She's still dealing with finding out Stu ain't her Daddy, well you know, I figured we'd wait to tell her about your part" he finished.

"Yeah well, that call...our daughter is with *my* godchild right now having a fit because she has a picture of me in an envelope from you, a man saying *he's her father* telling her *I'm her mother*" I finished.

"Sofiya, I just told my boys that I knew that I didn't have a baby with Celeste, I knew that for a fact but that was all I shared. If Jhonnie knows you're her mother, then she either got it from one of her brothers or she gathered it from whatever was in that bag" he concluded.

"Well, I'm going to talk to her, my flight leaves at noon" I grabbed my purse and gathered my things.

He looked at his watch, "I guess that means Ima have to come down there to finish what we started" he leaned down and kissed me.

Dammit, he is still it, but I couldn't look past his *vow of silence all these years.* I was guarded and very pissed at Dean, so, he had to feel it. I boarded my plane leaving him standing at the checkpoint, calling my phone asking me to stay.

"Another time, oh trust you'll be seeing me soon" I said before ending the call.

As I pulled out of the parking garage of the airport, I drifted into the memory of my life back during that time.

I feel like it's about time y'all heard my side of this story. At least an explanation of how we got to this point. I won't take you too far back. I'm not going to start from the beginning of my life, although *it's a very interesting story* or so I have been told. I'll just start from how I went from being the wife of one of the most well-known, to being an on the run expectant mother and girlfriend to another well-known guy in the life from a few towns over. All of this happened at the young age of twenty-five.

I am Sofiya (pronounced So-fee-ya) Robinson, and I was the wife of Joshua Bradshaw until his demise.

Joshua was thee guy to see, know and be connected to in or surrounding our town. I thought I had accomplished something because not only were we together; I was married to him. I was *Mrs. 'Bully' Bradshaw.*

I was young, still 'wet behind the ears', didn't know nothing type young and just dumb. I absolutely knew no better, coming from where I'm from. All I knew was Joshua was *the man, he was powerful, he was handsome as ever* and I wanted him.

The thing nobody warned me about and the question I should have been asking myself was, 'if he's the goon that gets *everybody* then who do we get to get him?'

Yeah, I didn't think about that until it was too late. I was already dug in.

I did find out the answer to that question, the hard way. Not only was he the one to get for the streets, but how bout Joshua was that *one* in his family. He was the one nobody wanted to piss off and he came from a family of goons. A real long line of "Mack Mittens".

My dumb self was just so proud to have him, until I couldn't get away from him. And trust me I tried to leave him, so many times. All of them were dramatic episodes. A few are documented in a county clerk's drawer, there's a record of arrest with my picture but not for my name. I learned a few things along the way, *I ain't stay dumb.*

But let me backup and describe that time I realized *the hard answer*, it was the first time I woke up with a fractured wrist, a bruised lip and no one to call. That's when I knew, but I was dug in, so I decided, I won't ever be that girl to just get hit. Bully knew I wasn't a lightweight, so he never tried me in public. We kept our fighting private. I know, that didn't make it better, but nevertheless I'm here to tell the tale.

Now, Joshua and I had fought many times before, but not like this. I mean *this was a fight!* I remember standing in front of him after turning from the mirror looking at how he busted my lip when he smacked me because I changed the locks *after* he stayed out for two nights.

I was glaring at him through teary eyes just being tired of him and his shit. I remember sucking my lips and saying. "Bully, I might lose this fight, but *pussy* it ain't gon be an easy win for you. Folks gon know you went a few rounds with me" I said before kicking off my shoes.

That was the last thing I remembered saying before all hell broke loose. Joshua charged at me, I picked up a lamp and threw it full force over my head at him. It was on from there; we began to tear each other up and rearrange our house in the process.

Joshua kept trying to grab me, but I learned his trick, so I kept moving and giving him body work. Whenever Bully is losing or getting winded, he likes to choke a bitch sleep.

It was just us in the house, so there was no one there to break us up. Lord knows I was wishing somebody was here because I was in what felt like a brawl for it all, I was literally fighting for my life.

"Stop tryna choke me Bully" I swatted my hands at him.

I somehow escaped his hold and punch him in his eye. I ran towards the stairs and do you know this bastard pushed me *up the stairs* and the fight continued in the hallway.

I remember fighting hard in that hallway, we knocked over pictures and broke a few pieces of art in our tussle. I kept telling myself, *you gotta* keep fighting. It was getting hard, but I would pause to catch my breath then go at him again. This went on for a few minutes until he grabbed me, and everything went black.

The next day when I woke up, I laid there trying to recall the last thing I remembered. I took a series of breaths before I opened my eyes.

I remember Bully was on top of me, after he threw me into the wall, knocking the wind outta me. I slid to the floor and he must have choked me out.

I had to been tearing his ass up...

I sat up and blinked my eyes while looking around the room. I made it! Yes, I woke up in pain but I'm here.

My whole body hurt, especially my wrist. However, my levels of pain were nothing like Bully's. I had aches, pains with some bruises and a busted lip. He had scratches, cuts, open wounds on top of the aches and pain.

Let me tell you, hearing his groans and moans as he walked to the bathroom was music to my ears for at least two days.

As I began putting the house back together, the following day, Joshua for the first time apologized for the night before and he promised never to hurt me like *that* again.

And for a long time, he didn't but after a while *Jerkbag Joshua's behavior* began to spiral in the same areas that caused our last fight, he started cheating again.

*Yes, he had the nerve to attack me b*ecause I was tired of him stepping out on me. I told him, 'If I wake up by myself then that's how I'm gonna stay' and he didn't believe me until I proved my point. He had to go through a lot to get in that house that night.

But back to his reckless behaviors, Joshua's belligerent attitude got worse, he was very disrespectful with his extracurricular activities with the local chicks around town.

As I said, I was young *and dumb,* so when I'd run down on him and his women in public, especially around town, I'd beat the brakes off them whores.

I sure did, people thought it was about him. Naw it was about the disrespect because every local chick *knew* I was his wife. Not his girlfriend, not some random, his wife. I married Joshua when I was nineteen years old, met him at sixteen. I was twenty-four, by now chile I was tired of his bullshit.

One would think him having to walk out in the streets with not only a puffy black knot under his eye, but he had three 'get off me' scratches across his pretty boy face, he would chill.

Nope, his boys tried to warn him as he walked around with a shiny face because he coated it with Vitamin E to prevent scaring.

"Bully, you betta chill! Ya wife ain't no joke" they warned.

But did he listen? Of course, Joshua Bradshaw didn't listen, he just began being more cautious with his shenanigans. He'd do stuff like drive hours just to go to the movies, dinner or other stuff outside of town with these same in-town chicks, so word of his adventures always made its way back to me.

I remember one time my cousin called me to let me know Joshua was at a dinner theater up the highway. I quickly got dressed and jumped in my car, ready for it. I didn't pick up anybody for the ride, I wanted to see him for and by myself, just in case.

I pulled up to the theater and that's when I almost threw up in my mouth. Joshua comes walking out of the theater with Celeste Bender!

'Really Joshua, Celeste????'

I fought the urge to go fuck up her life again. I had beat this bitch out her clothes, dragged her down the stairs and threw her out onto my lawn, on three separate occasions. I felt super disrespected, one because it was Celeste but for two, Joshua never circled back to the same chick.

"I already dragged this hoe, I'm tired of this heffa" I said aloud watching them walk to the car.

He really has feelings for this girl...

I want to fight, *not* because I want him, but just because I was so disgusted. Really though...*Celeste?*

In the past, me being dumb and Joshua being my husband, I believed him when he said they meant nothing, plus like I said, it was never the same one.

It was probably because Celeste was easy and her dumb ass would do anything he told her too, even sleep with other men for the setup. Yeah, I heard about that *in traffic.*

I knew Joshua loved to have sex and I knew it to be amazing, which was his issue. He was very good at that and *fucking shit up.* But as good as his sex was, I didn't want it.

I had been on the receiving end of him, *fuckin' shit up'* so much so that he didn't do it for me. I wasn't giving him any, so I was cool with him having whores.

Yes, do your thing but they gotta go home sweetie. Don't be tryna build nothing with these broads. We already have things in motion but that's a whole 'notha story for an entirely different day.

"This damn Celeste, I see a beating means nothing to her" I was beyond vexed.

Not only had I been asking Joshua to take me to this place for months, he had been throwing every excuse not to go. This asshole's latest excuse was, "It's too far for a movie' but you take *her?"* I said to myself, fuming at the bullshit.

The more I watched him walk and talk, the more it became clear. I decided; I was over my life with Bully.

"Man, I don't even have a fight anymore" I said turning off the highway leaving them to go wherever. I knew it was time to work on my exit strategy, but I planned to return the favor and fuck Celeste's dude before I go.

"Who's her main squeeze" I thought out loud. I put my feelers out to find her booski.

It's time for me to play...

A few weeks later, I saw Celeste in the mall with a dude, who I later found out was named Dean from Up Norf. That's how they told me I had to pronounce it, there's no *th* it's an *f.*

He was a super sexy young man. He was about six feet tall, he had wavy hair with thick eyebrows, strong cheekbone structure and full lips and best of all. He was from 'out of town'. This young man was definitely out of Celeste's league, and I was going to let him know it the first chance I got.

It was the third time I'd seen the two of them together. I didn't see them together, as much as I saw her, but they were definitely an item of some sort.

Now let me say this, Celeste wasn't ugly, she just didn't have *it*. Like her style was corny, she couldn't touch me on my worst and her best day, I think that's why I was so insulted at seeing Joshua taking this duck out in public. You don't give corny chicks them type privileges, you keep their tragic ass under wraps or indoors.

Listen, I'm no hater, like I said Celeste wasn't ugly, but she was just so messy and corny, I never understood how she had some of the best dudes in the game chasing her. I know you read some time back that this hoe had *my Bully* being disrespectful.

It was a lot, but I could have easily killed two birds with one stone. I could tag Celeste's ass for her bullshit and go for Joshua's jugular by just accepting one of the many "let me change your life" invites that I receive from *Abdul every time he sees me out.*

Abdul was one of the only guys in town that paid Bully and his spoiled boy antics no mind.

Abdul was the right-hand man to Bully's older brother, Justin before he was killed. With the family's blessing Abdul ventured off into his own thing. Now Bully was his competition, but I already knew how he looked at *JoshyPu.*

JoshyPu is what his mother calls him. Hold on, before I go any further, please know I rolled my eyes with all of my might after I mentioned his mother. That woman is a whole 'notha story.

I was rebellious but I knew messing with Abdul would get me kilt! No really Bully despised him so I'm not trying to die right now.

Maybe, just maybe, I'm ready for another few rounds of good *ole back of the limousine type fighting* before I go, but my goal is TO LEAVE...NOT DIE!

I avoided Abdul with all my might and lived another day. Ab was a problem, I kindly put him in my pocket for later. Now Dean, he was safe, so I put my focus on him.

I never knew when I would see Dean, so I made sure when I was frequenting any part of town, I was "in line and on time" meaning everything was right and I was looking like I was going somewhere. I'd be very overdressed for my market runs.

My makeup was beat, my manicure/pedicure was tight. I had cut my hair, so I wore pin curls which stayed looking like I just had them done because my hair girl taught me how to do them on myself to maintain my hair between my visits.

'I'm taller than your average woman, and I don't think I own a pair of sneakers. I always wear shoes and very rarely will I wear flats. I'm a girly girl but I like to be a little bit of a tomboy 'at home', especially when I'm moving around in them *backstreets*.

But when it comes down to outside of town??? Oh, I'm always sharp in *those* streets. Folks that knew me, know I can be a humorous, real chill type of lady that always tries to be good to people.

I don't do much, I bother nobody, and I mind the business that pays me. Normally, I'm the one that everyone loves, even the ones that hate my husband. This included his own circle, which was the majority of his family.

The Bradshaw's loved Sofiya, with exception of his mother, one brother and a few aunts and female cousins; them jealous bitches. And I say that because to all of his uncles and grandfather and other male family...I was still their Fi-Fi.

Now, not all of the female Bradshaw's took issue with me, some knew Bully to be too much. They knew I was growing tired of him. I drew this conclusion after I had been caught out a few towns over enjoying myself, and when I didn't have to fight with Bully about it, I knew I was cool. They hadn't reported back anything on me, but I still changed my flow to frequent another part of town and Dean's hangout areas.

It was a Friday night and I had made plans to stay in. My cousin Sabrina kept calling me from the bar around her way. I had forgotten she moved closer to Dean's side of town.

"Yo boy in here" she said as soon as I answered.

"Say word..." I jumped off my bed.

I had promised my girls the next time I saw Dean, I was gon make my move. "Shut up, is dum-dum there too?" I asked walking into the closet.

Sabrina confirmed, "mmm hmmm, but so what come on" she hung up the phone.

I turned on the music in my closet, "What color am I doing tonight" I scrolled through the stations until I heard "Square Biz" by my girl Teena Marie.

I threw my 'fit across the bed, retied my scarf, stripped out of my clothes and stepped into the shower as I prepared to go start some trouble.

I stepped into my blue Christian Louboutin's with the matching bag. I slid my arms into my leather jacket and wrapped a scarf around my neck.

I walked outside to my car and saw I had a flat tire, Joshua had called while I was getting ready, so he knew I was going out. This petty asshole really went out of his way to come by the house just to slash my tires.

"Oh, he gon play this game" I said feeling irritated but even more motivated to carry out my mission.

I walked back inside and called a cab. I stood in the hallway staring at myself in the mirror. I fixed my hair as I convinced myself *I had* to go! I knew once I got there, I could get home.

"See, he thinks, I think I'm too good for cabs, jokes on you buddy" I giggled as I walked outside.

I walked past slashing the other two tires. "Now it's disabled, I'll call the insurance people tomorrow. He'll be paying for that" I smirked.

I opened the door and climbed into my ride. *He stops nothing, I'm done being nice, he better hope I don't run into Abdul, he has been on my heels lately* and it's starting to feel like a good night to say, 'fuck it'.

I walked into Choppy's lounge and guess whose face was the very first face I saw standing by the bar? Yup, Mister Sexy Man of the hour himself.

'Yup, I think Ima have him take me home' I thought to myself.

I looked at him again as I hugged my cousin. He had his back towards me, but then he turned around and our eyes met. I noticed he took a minute to look away, Dean smiled at me.

"Yea, he's definitely taking me home" I yelled to my cousin over the loud music as we walked to the bar.

I spent the next half hour flirting with him from across the room for a couple songs. We played that game a few more beats before he finally came over to speak to me.

I had already learned Dean was just another street guy but talking to him, he's giving me more of a legit cross-over type vibe. I played uninterested when he began to tell me his 'claim to fame' because I didn't really care about his life at that point. I was more focused on getting Celeste to know I was 'bout to '*yank*' her man. Shit, she had mine! Matter fact, she's with him now, I looked at my watch. She must have cut out to meet him before I got here.

Dean ordered me another drink as he stood behind me talking over my shoulder into my ear. Of course, the song was extra sexy. I caught Celeste's friend Evelyn staring at me, so I laughed a little harder at his jokes and leaned into him a little bit more. I was just about to ask Dean about taking me home when Shizz walked in.

Shawn aka Shizz was part of Joshua's crew, one of his close homeboys that I knew before he got caught up in the life.

Recently, Shizz had been whispering about doing his own thing. Shizz did his rounds in the bar before he made his way over towards me, "Feeya" Shizz smirked.

Shizz nodded his head as he extended one hand to Dean as a greeting. He reached past him with the other to grab me under my arm, "Lemme talk to you" he said not giving me a chance to object.

Shizz walked me down the bar, "Yo, you're trippin" he said not beating around any bushes.

I put my hand on my chest, "What did I do" I smiled as I sipped my drink.

"Do you know how many calls I got 'bout you and Skate being all chummy" he pointed at Dean.

"Oh, is that what y'all call him" I smiled and turned to look at Dean.

On cue, Dean smiled and raised his drink in my direction.

Shizz put his hand on my shoulder and turn me back to face him, "I'm being fa real Sa'feeya" he said letting his country accent push through.

I twisted my face up confused, "And what you do mean calls?" I asked.

He nodded, "calls…yes plural as in more than one" Shizz replied.

I shook my head, "Folks should really mind their business, I wonder how many calls you get when Jackass be carting and tricking on these hoes around here" I circled the room with my finger.

Shizz ignored my question but advised me that because I looked out for him many times before, he wasn't going to rat me out but warned me to be careful because my friendliness with Skate almost got back to Bully.

Fast forward nearly a year later, picture me with both my middle fingers completely in the air at my husband. I didn't give a damn about Bully finding out anything about me.

Pack up ya stuff Mr. DJ, the party was over, I was so done with him, you hear me? I was done with his bullshit; his double standard and I was over him parading these hoes in my face like dudes ain't coming after ya girl, damn near every day. Even Abdul voiced his feelings of disappointment that I chose Dean to be the one.

"Word is born, Dean Murphy? Not hating on that man but when you finally decide to come off the porch, you choose a Murphy?" he said staring at me in the parking lot.

Abdul caught up to me coming out of the nailery. By this time, Dean and I were a real thing. We had been on trips, we had weekly meetups and we talked daily. I was being cautious just for the sake of not wanting people in my business. I didn't give a damn about how it made anyone else feel.

I used to switch Dean's name in my phone just in case Bully decided to care and check my phone, even though he claims *'going through a woman's phone or purse'* is a sucka ass move...

Dean started out as 'Johnnie on da Spot' my mobile mechanic because not only was he great at maintaining me, but he also had real deal car connections.

The way it would work was I would get to a destination and I would call for roadside assistance whenever I wanted to meet. Then, a tow truck would come get me and my car then take me to another destination, where he'd be waiting, and we'd ride out in his tinted Audi coupe.

At first, the whole professional, 'I'm calling to bring my car in for service' backed Joshua up off me. But then he started asking questions, so I just switched up.

One time he almost caught me, but I quickly jabbed my way out of that corner, "You're not doing some sucka ass, pussy ass moves like going through my phone are you?" I asked smirking knowing he would never admit to such an act.

Of course, he denied it, he just backed up off me while saying my name in a sing-songy type of way. "So-fee-yaaa, keep thinkin' shit sweet" he said.

I should have known then he was next level crazy, but he relaxed a little, so I just thought I played it *safer*.

Dean became "Nay' my nail girl" in my phone. That was short lived because I guess I was scheduling appointments for my nails and car maintenance a little too much for Joshua's liking. He was becoming a bit suspicious, so much so that I think he had people following me.

All of this from a man that says he don't care...

It started getting strange, I would catch him doing stuff like Joshua used to secretly smell me. Not my lady parts or nothing like that because we had been stopped having sex. He'd smell my arms, my boobs, my collarbone, etc. You know the places where my body could possibly touch another mans. I really didn't understand why he cared, he had a bunch of bitches, and Celeste was surely not the only one.

One day I had just finished meeting with Dean at the hotel when Joshua met me in the parking lot. I walked around the building to see him sitting on my car waiting for me. I knew it was about to be some shit when he didn't say anything. Up to this point, Joshua had stopped giving me money. I had been "cut off" but Momma ain't miss no meals.

As I've said before, I didn't understand why he cared. So, imagine my surprise when Joshua hopped down off my car and threw money in my face and told me to 'get my mind right'.

I looked down at the money on the ground, "Keep your lil money" I snarled my face up at him as I tried to step over it to get to my car.

And that's when old Joshua da Jackass came out, the twist was Joshua had never put his hands on me in public, but I guess at this point, he didn't care.

"You're gonna take this money and you're gonna fix it!! Or you're dead to me" Joshua said through clenched teeth and practically foaming at the mouth, his eyes looked crazy.

This wasn't regular sober, but angry Josh; this was that same high outta his jackass mind Bully, that almost killed me that night. I thought to myself as my stomach tightened and I prepared myself for the fight.

This jerk back hand slapped me so hard, I don't know what happened but something inside clicked and I had *had* enough! I snapped and started swinging my arms connecting with his body and face.

Joshua clenched my hair in his fist, he raised his hand and I swung up and kept swinging as I turned to face him.

"Get the fuck off me Josh" I yelled

I felt wetness on my hands and chest. While he was shaking and choking me, I had opened the blade on my keys and sliced him with it. I don't even know how many times, but I knew his ass was leaking.

Bully stumbled back, he swayed side to side then fell to his knees. I pushed off against the wet ground and began running to my car while he was trying to get his bearings together.

I turned to see him pull out his gun. I started the car and got out of there, but not before Bully shot out two of my windows, one being the rear window and my back passenger window when I turned out of the parking lot.

This bastard was really shooting at me!?!?!?

I went to a few places that night, first stop was I swapped cars. I couldn't chance driving around without a window and get pulled over, especially since no one was answering their phones.

I drove directly to Shizz's babymom's house when he didn't answer my calls or his door. I called Dean but his phone went straight to voicemail. I sat in my car watching her place, I think she had guests over so I couldn't just go inside, especially since in all the commotion I failed to acknowledge that I was covered in blood.

I was cool with waiting for Shizz to come out. Yolanda aka Shug, Shizz's babymom came out by herself and left in one of his other cars.

All this time and he wasn't there? Well, that just pissed me off.

"Now, where you going?" I said out loud, as I followed behind her to a warehouse way out somewhere.

Imagine my surprise when I saw Shizz open the bay doors and Yolanda drove inside.

"What the heck is this place" I said looking around as I pressed the button to call Shizz and it didn't ring but the voicemail came on.

I called Dean again. *Shit!!!!* I yelled at his voicemail coming on.

I threw the phone down and I was about to leave when I saw the lights from a truck coming up the road. I watched a truck pull-up to unload some stuff then pulled back out. I continued watching the warehouse until Yolanda left again, but this time she wasn't alone.

I was tired of waiting. I needed to know what the hell was going on, plus I needed to know if Shizz heard anything about Joshua.

Please God, let him be okay...even though he's an asshole, I don't want him dead. I'm not trying to go to prison. More importantly, my nosy ass wants to know what the hell they got going on out here.

I got out of the car and walked across the field. I looked in the window and was prepared to knock on the door, but my knees went weak. I think the gun pointed at the back of my head and hearing it cock is what made me quickly begin to apologize while pleading for my life.

"Sa' feeya, da fuck is you doing out hurr?" he asked.

I don't think I had ever been so happy to hear Shizz's country ass voice.

Shizz dropped his gun and pulled me inside the warehouse doorway by my collar. "What happened to you, whose blood is this?" he asked.

I turned to look and caught a glimpse of myself in the glass, "Oh my God what did I do" I panicked and fell into hysterics.

I don't remember too much after that, but I do recall Yolanda walking in the warehouse, coming to get me.

She put me in the car, and we rode in silence to their house, I had to duck down in the back as she drove into her garage.

"Ok come on" she said as she opened my door.

I was sitting in a daze when I felt something pulling on me. I looked over at her and when I looked into her eyes something cracked and I began to cry. And I mean I cried hard.

"Why, like *this* can't be my life, how did this happen?" I asked.

I continued to cry as Yolanda tried to console me. She helped me out of the car and into the house, then guided me through her home into the bathroom.

"Here, take a shower and put these on. You'll feel better" she handed me some clothes.

I sat on the bench in front of her tub, and she helped me take my clothes off.

"If anybody asks me, you were here all night" she said.

I looked at her, "Yolanda" I said, and she turned to look at me.

I considered asking her some questions, but I opted to wait. "Thank you" I smiled at her. I picked up the washcloth and towel, "Do you have some shampoo and stuff for my hair?" I asked and she nodded.

"I'll get you some" Yolanda walked out the bathroom and opened a closet. I stepped into the shower and adjusted the water. Yolanda handed me some products and turned on some music then left the bathroom.

I lost myself in that shower. I cried as I thought about my life.

I thought about Shizz and that warehouse. I thought about Dean and the "nobody that turned out to be *his wife*.

Yes, after all of *that*, Dean was married! And not that it mattered because so was I but at least he knew. That was one of the things we were discussing when Joshua ran down on me.

Shit, here I was thinking Celeste was the one, and this man is married with children. But in my defense, I don't know what kinda setup they had going on because Dean has spent days into weeks at a time with me. Whenever Joshua went out of town on "business", so the fuck did I and guess who was with me? You guessed it!

And I don't mean just quick little weekend overnights or getaways out of town. No, I mean like, we took a ten-day vacation with a five-day cruise before. We've been to Paris and Puerto Rico. I've been to his grandmother's house while we were in Barbados.

And we've visited all these places in a time span of like nine months. So, as I stand in this shower crying about my husband trying to kill me, that wasn't even what had me vexed. I was more upset about my boyfriend having a wife and was even more annoyed because he's not answering his phone.

One thing I did know for certain, I knew I had to kick "Operation Great Escape" into effect like right now all by myself if need be because Dean, my married ass boyfriend ruined the original plan.

"Are you ready" Shug asked yanking me from thoughts of my past.

"This is my first time seeing her since I've talked to Dean" I said looking out the window.

"What did he say about all this" Shug asked walking over to the door.

"That's a whole 'notha story for an entirely different day" I sighed.

So, this is where we are now? They don't even know I've planned for this! I hope they're ready!

Chapter 17 Rhyon:

They call me Sir Brother Fetta...

I don't think anyone realizes how much stress it can be growing up with a bunch of females in your family. I'm my momma's only child but I have a brother, we share the same father. Even though I was her only child, I was never the only child in our house growing up. There was always a cousin or two living with us. My mother had to raise my two girl cousins, Missy and Brandi, after their mother was drugged and never quite recovered.

Missy and Brandi were nearly teenagers when they came one weekend and never left because their mom was found in an abandoned car. They had lived with us for over six years.

I had another cousin that was also like a sister, we called her Stink. And just like Brandi and Missy, Stink spent a lot of time at our house. My mother couldn't stand my uncle's on again/off again girlfriend, turned wife Celeste. They fought at every turn, my mom made it a point to go out of her way to always keep my cousin for however long without consulting her mother; especially, during those times when Unc was locked up. Eventually, Celeste stopped fighting and Stink was able to come and go from my mom's house as she pleased.

Damn, my bad! I'm explaining my family and I didn't even introduce myself. My name is Rhyon Demby aka Fetta. It's a nickname that started at home, then spread to the hood. My mom called me *Fella, but my younger cousins* said *Fetta,* and it stuck.

Then the running joke was I'm the *horrible combination of a Dad and a big brother,* so the girl cousins started calling me Sir Brother Fetta. We'll get into how that name spread like wildfire later.

But back to me, I'm the only child of Delphine, and she's one the last of the Demby siblings. It was seven of them, she was the first girl and older sister to Stanley aka Stuy Money from Out da Bay. He only has one child, that's my sister-cousin Stink, y'all may also know her as Jhonnie. The cousins aren't sure who gave her the name Stink, but that was her name to us.

It's crazy how drama always erupts in our family around either a funeral, baby or a wedding. The last episode was right before Jhonnie left for school and one of my uncles was killed on the road. He had a lot going on at one time and it all was revealed in the days leading up to his services.

At his funeral, the women were arguing, and information started being tossed around. One of my uncle's girlfriend's shared how phony the family had been for knowing my uncle had *multiple children with different women* all the while, *keeping it quiet that he was still legally married.*

Our family barely survived that public embarrassment before the next scandal was exposed this time it was at my Uncle Stu's wake. He was the kinda guy everyone loved, while Ms. Celeste, his wife rubbed those same folks the wrong way.

She was a messy and mean lady, the type that always takes things too far. I personally didn't care for her just on the strength of how she treated Stink. I stopped calling her 'aunt' a long time ago, then my mom heard me one day and said I had better put a handle on it because she wasn't my friend. So, she quickly became Ms. Celeste.

I remember vividly telling my mother, "I don't want to call her aunt. I be annoyed when she sees me out and wants to make it known that I'm her nephew" I explained our last awkward interaction at the stadium.

"Listen, you don't get in this mess. This is adult shit, stay in your place" my mom replied.

"It's kinda hard to stay out of it when she keeps hurting my sister's feelings. She told Stink she's not her mom, so if she's not her mom, then she ain't my aunt" I quickly retorted.

"Who said that? Who said she's not Stink's mom?" My mother asked striking me with her serious tone.

"Stink said, she overheard Ms Celeste saying something along the lines of 'wishing she left her where she found her" I repeated the words to my mom.

I believe it was that comment that sent my mother on a journey for the truth because of course Ms. Celeste denied ever saying that. My mother knows I'm no liar, especially when it doesn't relate to me. My mom said she believed me, but I still felt bad because that caused a major rift between my mom and my Uncle Stuy for a while.

I was kinda relieved when the same lady that showed out at my Uncle Dukie's funeral shared, since it was Ms. Celeste that revealed Uncle Dukie had a wife. She felt the need to return the favor by asking Ms Celeste a question at her man's funeral. Of course, she asked it in *ear shot of my mother*.

"So, did Stuy know the truth about Stink not being his or yours for that matter?" she asked fanning herself.

I don't think it was that question that fucked my mom's head up, I think it was the question that put Ms Celeste's back against the wall.

My mom turned around and said, *"Oh* yeah he knew. Now go head Celeste answer Reenie's question because now I want to know, "Where's this boy?" she asked.

Ms. Celeste was stuck, so she started a scene that drew a crowd, knowing my mom would let it go and she did, but I didn't. I drove straight to my mom's house after the services. I needed answers, but once I got them, I wish I had of let it go.

My grandmother used to say, '*It ain't always good to know!'*

*And s*he ain't never lied because *knowing* has been hell on me and Stink's relationship ever since I found out the truth about her parents.

Of course, she noticed my attitude change, I had been avoiding our weekly meetups for quite some time. I couldn't look in her face, knowing what I knew and *not* tell her, so I took the easy way out, and ducked her. I chose to show up places after she already left, or I'd leave when she was on the way.

I had been successful with avoiding Stink, which wasn't easy to do because since we were little, it was always, us. Whether it was me, Stink and Brandi or me, Missy and Stink, she was somewhere close to me. In fact, she's guaranteed to be in any picture someone has of me. Stink is my number two rollie. She's only number two because it was me and Missy for a few years before Stink came. Missy calls it her *seniority*.

In age, Stink is between us and Brandi, she made it not so weird having Brandi around because she was younger. It's definitely more fly, now that we're all grown.

Because our parents were *in the life;* with exception of my mom, my cousins and I were afforded the opportunity for a better life than most. We all graduated college and decided to open a business together. Right now, Stink doesn't do anything hands-on, she's just an investor to our company. She was going through some legal situations, but she walked up out thing on top.

I'm an architectural engineer, Missy is a mortgage broker and Brandi is our CFO/finance banker girl. We do consultation work on the side for upcoming business. Missy made a few of the girl cousins get their real estate licenses and they're working on making their own boutique, type realty thing.

My family was doing well, even Stink had recovered from her legal debacle and found a new job in her old stomping grounds. She wasn't interested in all that we were doing, so she chose to get a job.

Stink hated it because it was a huge drop in salary but she had somehow acquired a commercial building with residential setup in the property so her means could take the cut.

Okay, lemme not get too far off track...let me catch y'all up. So, I'm ducking Stink but not for what she thinks. She thinks I'm mad at her messing around with one of them Murphy's, but I learned he ghosted her. Plus, she was on to the next guy, so that ain't the reason.

Naw, I fucked around and had a threesome with one of her cousins and *some chick she knows* through this new dude she keeps dipping in and outta town with...yeah that's a whole 'notha story.

The reason I'm going to my mom's was to get my carry-on I had stashed over there two weeks ago when my lady, Kabira popped up. She was meeting up with the girl cousins and wanted to drive my truck so they could go in one vehicle.

My girl didn't know I floated outta town that weekend. I had to smuggle my carry-on out of the car before they left. I slid it to the side door and my mom's friend put it in my old room.

Now that I'm being requested outta town again and I need my bag. I drove to my mom's. I parked after I circled the block, just making sure I ain't see a familiar car because remember now, *I'm duckin' Stink!*

I knew I was on a timer, so I hurried up across the street to get the bag and keep it moving.

I walked into the house, "Ey Ma, where you at?" I yelled as I locked her screen door.

She appeared in the hallway at the top of her stairs. "Fetta, what are you doing here I don't even have the energy for you. I just got off the phone with Stink" she flagged her hand and walked back into her room.

I started to go up the stairs when someone tapped on the door and tried to open it, but it was locked.

I looked at the door, "*Shiitt*, well you better find it because Stink here and she don't look happy" I whisper yelled at my mom as I backed down the stairs and unlocked the screen door.

"Shit! Okay..." my mother whispered from her room getting up.

"Oh, look who it is! Well, if it isn't, Mr. Where da fuck you been?" she said with her funny sarcastic voice.

I pulled her into a hug, "Cut that out, I've been busy. I got this project at work and I just got back from outta town, I gotta get ready to go back" I explained.

Stink cut me off, "Rhy-on *shut the fu...boy!*" she raised her hand then pointed at me.

"Why have you been duckin' me? Do you owe me money?" she asked looking at her phone.

I thought real quick, "I do actually, but that's not why I been duckin' you, *shit*" *I said.*

"Ah Haaa, so you admit it!! Ant Dell, I told y'all! Sir Brother Fetta been duckin' me" she announced.

Damn, she got me! I'm too used to being comfortable with my cousin. I don't usually hide stuff from her.

"Leave him alone Stink" my mom said coming down the stairs to my rescue.

My mom closed the front door then picked up her stick off the wall. Stink broke out in laughter, "Ant Dell stop playing" she ran around the couch avoiding my mother from getting close enough to her to give her *a pow pow*.

"Come here now, I ain't gon chase you. I told you if you came here, I was gon' pop you. So, come on *get over here*" she added some tension to her tone.

Stink dropped her arms then shrugged, "Well, come on with it because I'm not leaving here without some answers" she walked over and turned her backside to face my mother.

My mom papped her with her *pow pow* stick. That's what the kids call it. It's just a big paint stirrer on the wall and if the kids act up, she'll add your name to it. Then the next time, she'll just point to it and they'll get back in line.

Only thing is, in my mom's eyes, *you're never too old to get popped when you come in her house* that stick was decorated with names from years ago.

"Ok, so what was worth you coming all the way out here?" my mom asked turning on the lights in her dining room.

Stink went into her oversized bag and pulled out two envelopes. She held them up, "So, I had a visitor that gave me these" she said.

Stink sat down as she began to explain to us what had been going on these past few months that we hadn't seen or talked to each other.

"So yeah, that's what I've been dealing with" she announced falling back into her seat.

I looked at my mom, not giving her a chance to reply. I figured I'd buy her some time. I got up from my seat and walked over to my cousin. I took Stink by her hands, "Come 'ere man" I said pulling her up.

"My bad, I was being selfish not even thinking. I was caught up in my own shit, that I wasn't there for you, can you forgive me?" I asked.

Stink just fell into my chest, I held onto my cousin as she cried.

She's not used to showing her emotions in front of certain folks, so even though it was just me and my mom, her strong ass danced me into the kitchen to have a more private cry.

I stood in the doorway blocking my mother's view as she turned her back and cried some more.

"I thought you were doing me how my other cousins did me, you know after my Grandmom Ann passed" she sniffed and huffed trying to catch her breath.

I dropped my head at the memory of how her cousins treated her after Ms. Celeste's mother passed, "Look at me" I directed her as I turned her around by her shoulders.

I waited until she looked up, "I don't give a damn what any of those papers in that bullshit ass envelope says...you're *my* family! My cousin, my rollie and I never liked her as your mom anyway so..." I shrugged as Stink fell on me laughing, which made me stop talking to join her.

"No for real, I'm not even calling her Ms. Celeste anymore, *no!* I don't even want to hear her name so, *from now on she's the woman formerly known as my uncle's wife"* I said.

"Say what now?" my mother yelled from the table.

"Nothing" we yelled back from the kitchen.

Stink kissed my mom's forehead, then threw a peace sign over her head. "Not that this isn't fun, but I have to go get ready to go outta town again" she announced.

I decided since me and Stink was back on top, I figured I'd hold off on letting my suspicions be known regarding who exactly her *new thing* was, I know her and Rash been messing around. They swear they low, but I peeped their side conversations at Brandi's housewarming. Then all of a sudden, Rash is spending time Up Top.

Matter fact, he recently bought another place right *after selling a place* saying he was *done with Up Norf.*

I'll get to the bottom of it. I'll see what I find out when I go outta town this weekend.

"You know I didn't even come over here for all this" I announced walking into my old room to grab my carryon.

"Oh no?" my mom asked as she cut and wrapped me up some cake to go.

"Naw, not at all. I *had* been duckin' Stink" I chuckled at me telling on myself.

"So yeah, wasn't prepared for all that" I said joking.

"Well then I don't know how to tell you this but..." my mom's voice cracked.

I walked around the corner to lay eyes on my mother. "Ey Ma, you ai'ight?" I asked walking into the kitchen.

My mom turned around, took the kitchen towel off her shoulder, covered her face and cried. She cried so hard; she was bent over just sobbing into the towel.

"Aye Ma, what the hell" I said holding her up.

After she finally calmed down, she looked up at me. "I'll tell you, but Rhyon you have got to promise me..." she started to say.

I cut her off knowing this was *secret secret* type information. My mom never calls me Rhyon unless she's serious.

My mom and I are close, I know her gears and quirks so, I can tell when she called me by name, she was serious.

Not to mention, she let me call her Gladys several times as I helped her to a seat.

Gladys is the old lady name I gave her when she said I can't ever call her Delphine, not even playing. I guess she was cool with Gladys.

After hearing my mom's *secret secret,* I got up and grabbed her bottle of Brandy off the counter. I poured a shot and took it down with no chaser. I looked at my mom, I started to talk but I couldn't formulate a complete thought, so I just poured another shot.

"Where's Kabira?" she asked at my fourth shot.

I shrugged, "And Mom, please don't call Birry, I don't want her here...please just don't call her" I quickly threw down two more shots while I half answered my mother's questions.

I looked at my mom, "She's not talking to me right now, I beat up her boss and she might lose her job" I said then grabbed a beer out of her fridge.

My mom jumped up and grabbed a bag, "Oh lord Fetta, eat this" she shoved a Hawaiian roll into my hand.

I objected and tried to give it back, "But I don't want it" I said.

"Dammit, Fetta eat it..." she demanded.

I unwillingly ate that delicious ass roll. I'll tell her another day that she saved my life and how I ate two more without her knowing, but for now, that can wait.

I walked over to the living room and flopped down, "Whatchu call this thing again?" I asked with my eyes closed.

"A fainting couch, Fetta" she replied in an agitated tone.

"Yeeaa, a *fainting couch, how fitting"* I let out a heavy sigh as I fell back against it.

"So, you told them 'bout my Dad? And how he ain't dead?" I asked my mom sitting up looking at her.

"No Fetta, but I'm waiting on him to call me back. I left word for him" she came over and stood next to me.

I looked up at my mom, "And you're sure he's my brother?" I asked.

My mother nodded her head, "I'm waiting for confirmation now" she said.

"Ay yie yie" I said as I took my hat and put it over my face as I fell back on her *fainting couch*.

"So, they suspended you?"

I heard my mom talking to someone, I opened my eyes to see the inside of my hat. I opted to continue playing sleep once I heard Kabira's voice coming out of the kitchen.

Kabira is tight with the girl cousins, she started out as Brandi's best friend since childhood, but now she's my Birry. That's my baby. Well, the one I claim but that's a whole 'notha story.

"Yea, I had to go meet with HR today" she said.

"Behind what happened between Fetta and that guy?" my mother asked loudly.

"Really Anty" Kabira said in an attempt to quiet her up.

"You would think that would've been discussed or mentioned but he'll never admit it, so they are attacking mistakes I made months ago. I'm being demoted in title but not money" she replied.

"Oh Birry, I'm so sorry! Huhn, come on and gimme" my mom hugged her.

"So that's why y'all not speaking?" my mother asked.

"Oh no, I was cool with Rhyon rag doll'n my supervisor's ass, *my bad*. What I wasn't and am still NOT OK WITH..." she yelled in my direction.

"Is Rhyon accusing me of cheating with my supervisor like he wasn't the one missing in action just two weeks ago" she concluded ratting me out to my mom.

I tried to get up when I heard my mom grab her stick off the wall, but my ass was a little drunker than I thought. I fell into her cabinet, knocking it over, breaking her dishes.

She still popped me, once she saw I wasn't cut or anything, *then* made me clean it up.

It's murder trying to concentrate when you're on one.

"Now Birry, I ain't know all that! I wouldn't have called you over here to get him. Ida made his drunk ass sleep it off" my mom announced.

I put my head down as I walked past my mother towards Kabira. "Can we talk?" I asked slurred my words as she followed/guided me to my old room.

I flopped on the bed, "Come 'ere Man" I pulled Kabira onto the bed. "I'm sorry, you gotta stop being mad at me. I didn't do nothing" I whined as I lied into her lap.

Truth was I did A LOT, maybe a little too much this time. This is also the reason that I'm ducking my cousin.

A little while back, I met this girl on one of my trips outta town. I'm thinking nobody knows me out here I can chill, and that's just what I did.

Life was good, well a year later, my cousin Brandi's job moves her to my 'outta town' getaway.

I should have found another spot and left this one alone when I heard Stink be out here because Stink is the social cousin, she knows some of everyone. Laying low coulda been easy but no my head is hard.

This last trip, some shit came out and let's just say, I gotta figure out how to keep my outta town mess, just *that* outta town as I try to get my baby to forgive me while staying off my cousin's radar because I already know she's telling if she finds out.

I was doing good too, right when I started feeling myself is when I realized this shit had the potential to go left real fast.

I was out of town, when this babe I used to float with back in the day, hit my phone for another meet-up. I was with it especially when I walked in and it was two of them.

Then we met again and this time it was three of them. Talk about wild times, I actually started feeling one more than the other so we would hang whenever I touched down. I'd even take her with me on other business trips. That was my boo on the low, so imagine my stomach dropping when Rash shared some information with me about how close to home this rendezvous had hit.

"You said her name was what?" Rash asked as he pulled away from the terminal. He picked me up when I got back in town.

"Which one?" I asked jokingly.

Rasheed nodded then gave a light chuckle, "The one you keep talking about, what's her name?" he continued focusing on the road.

"Oh, you mean my boo, the one I'm tryna take from my outta town girlfriend without my main thang finding out" I mentioned while turning the music down.

"Yeah, now how'd you meet her?" he asked.

"I met her on some hum bug type shit, I needed a cut for a last-minute meeting. The girl at the hotel referred me to this unisex salon, I walk in expecting a dude. Nope, it was Ness, which was short for Vanessa" I said finally revealing her name.

This was when he revealed my problem was bigger than I thought.

"Well let me be the one to tell you, I think you might want to add, *keep Stink and the other girl cousins off my ass* to ya list. If this is the same Ness that I think it is, she does Stink's hair, and they are mad cool like they hang out and shit" Rash shared.

"Oh yea? How you know?" I asked sarcastically giving him the side eye.

Rash chuckled as he dropped his head, "Well obviously, you know how I know" he replied.

"So, what's the real deal with you and Stink?" I asked as we pulled into the parking lot.

"Whatchu mean?" he asked trying to buy time.

"Come on, I saw her car parked in ya new hood last time she was in town" I shared then quickly added. "Y'all not low by the way...just saying. I peep shit too" I finished.

Rasheed dropped his head and chuckled lightly. "Me and Stink been chilling. We are keeping things light and low. Not low because of me, it's her because she still fuckin with this dickhead bul, Ski" he shared.

"Yea, I heard Ness talking to him on the phone before, he a needy ass dude. He's always calling Ness *needing* something" I shared.

Rasheed took a deep breath and shook his head.

"I thought you were over that once you heard about her having a dude?" I asked as I followed him into the store.

"Yeah man, tried that and was serious about it too" he looked over at me.

"But *it* happened! You tried to warn me, Sticks tried and hell even Pudd tried...but now that I'm in it, it's too late" he shared smirking.

"She got me, and I don't wanna leave her alone" he replied with a shrug.

"Well, ole needy ass dude knows she is messing with someone, he just don't know it's you" I shared.

"Fuck I care?" he replied sharply with a shoulder shrug.

"I mean, I'm hearing he's talking 'bout popping' up on Stink, just saying" I held my hands up.

"Maaann, he not. Trust me he not! If he come to Stink house, he gon have more than me on his ass. Send that word back through *ya boo*, a popup wouldn't be a good look for Ski" he said.

Dayummm, well that just changed the whole game. What the hell is my cousin doing that she got these dudes ready to throw it all away for her.

I was heading out West to chill with my lil brother when my mom called my phone. "Hey Fetta" she said.

I let her know I was driving but I was alone, so she was good.

"I got ya Dad on the line" she announced.

"Hey Son, how you?" his voice resonated through the phone.

"Yo Dad, I'm cool and you?" I asked.

My mother started to explain her reason for calling me. My dad wanted to be the one to tell me the truth. I listened to their exchange. My father had to go but he told me he'd see me soon, then he hung up.

"Fetta?" my mom called out.

"I'm here" I announced as I was still processing the information from my father.

"You okay? Are you alright?" my mom asked.

I scoffed at her question, "Am I alright? Are you alright? Ain't that ya friend?" I asked her.

My mother took an exaggerated breath then groaned, "Oh my goooddd, it's like a lotta layers to this shit" she said.

"Okay so, you can't say nothing. I mean it Rhyon" she said.

I put on my blinker to pull off into the nearest parking lot. I had no clue what my mom was about to share, but I felt like I needed to be planted.

"Ar'ight Ma, what is it now? I let out a breath as I put my car in park.

"I'm not mad because your Dad and I were on one of our many breaks, plus I can't be mad at my friend for that; especially because she's not his real mom" she said softly.

"Huh? Like what is you saying? Did anybody keep their kids? Like you are my mom, right? I mean they say we look alike but..." I chuckled trying to lighten her mood.

"Shut the hell up Rhyon" she said, and I could tell she had her lips curled as she spewed that through her teeth.

"Well do we know who his mother is?" I asked,

"Yup, and when your Dad gets here, he'll tell you everything" she replied.

I looked at my phone receiving the notification for another call. I pressed ignore, it was Stink. I'll call her back. I don't know why I thought she was gon chill because she didn't. I think it was her calling me five times then sending me a middle finger, then a fist then a bomb emoji that made me decide I needed to take her next call.

"Hey Ma, I'll call you back" I said before ending the call.

I took a deep breath before answering her, "Hey Stink" I smiled bracing myself for the ram.

"You just *not* gon do right huh?" she yelled into the phone.

"*Rhy-on,* you are the reason dot dot dot" she yelled into the receiver.

"What's the dot dot dot?" I asked trying not to laugh.

I know she was serious, but my cousin Stink is funny as hell. She's quick witted and random.

"The reason I don't love these hoes" she yelled.

"Oh, I'm the reason?!" I chuckled.

"Yes, you *are* the reason" she repeated.

"So, I'm the reason why the party at The Vine got closed down the other week right? That was me?" I asked.

I took her silence as a clue that she didn't think anyone heard. "Ugh, you get on my nerves. Listen, I was minding my business" she retorted.

According to Ness, her and Stink went out and she walked up on Rafiq out with another girl at brunch, she tore the whole place up and made Rafiq drive her home. Only to have her friend come pick her up from his house.

"How the hell do you know about that...I *know Brandi and Missy ain't tell you*" she replied trying to figure out how I knew.

"Don't worry 'bout how I know, you betta hope dickhead bul don't find out about Rash " I concluded.

"*Whatever Rhy-on, shut up!* And ain't nothing going to happen because me and Rash ain't even like that..." she unconvincingly lied.

"Ok well if you don't tell Birry bout me, then I won't discuss this misunderstanding around Rash" I offered hoping she wouldn't call my bluff.

"I'm not gon volunteer but I won't lie if I'm asked" she shared.

"Yea ai'ght and if you're asked you betta spin that shit to the best of your ability" I instructed.

"Listen, I gotta go Ima call you later" I ended the call as I pulled up to Ness' shop and she was standing outside with some folks.

I heard her light up when someone asked about my truck. Ness turned around and squealed, "Ahhhh, I'm 'bout to go break bread with my ole head, I'll see y'all" she smiled walking to my ride.

Damn I'm gon miss her...

"Hey Poopie Poops" she said happily hugging my neck.

She sat back in her seat and grabbed her seatbelt. I flipped my phone in her direction. "Oh, you look cute, wayment" she leaned closer to look at the picture.

"That's my boo Beanie, wait how do you know her? Please don't tell me *that's* your girlfriend" she asked putting her hands over her face.

"Nah, *Beanie,* is my cousin as in our parents are siblings type cousins. Like same last name type cousins" I said

Ness' reaction let me know she definitely knew how my cousin could be. "Lawd, I'd rather she was your girlfriend! Awww maannn, this just changes *everything"* she said.

Ness turned to me, "So then you know her brother, Pudd? You've seen him at the shop before, he be selling those treats. I bought you one you gotta remember him?" she asked.

I shook my head, "I mean I remember the treat, but I don't remember him, and Stink don't have no brother's. Damn, wait yes she do" I said remembering Stink just shared that she learned she got brothers from her biological father.

"So, I guess this is it. You're still my ole head, we just can't break bread anymore" Ness said smiling.

"Oh, you already know, you're always gon be my baby" I kissed her forehead.

"So, I've been telling you stuff all this time, and that's your cousin? You know they're engaged right?" she arched her eyebrows and opened her door. "Ooooo, maybe not" she chuckled as she climbed out the car.

I decided to sit on this information. Hmmmm, I wonder if Rash knows about this here engagement.

I bet that'll keep her spinning the focus off me. Plus, I'm ending things with Ness so I'm good, or so I thought.

Chapter 18: Jhonnie

The bullsh*t...

I walked into work the next day very early and ready for the bullshit. I already knew Darcy wanted to do site visits with me. I'd been dreading them all month.

I walked into my cubicle and opened my desk drawer to get my Clorox wipes. I wiped down my phone, keyboard and mouse. I sprayed my keyboard and opened my new desk fragrance that Amira got for me. I lifted my calendar and saw an envelope with her handwriting on it.

"I love her" I opened the card and put my hand on my heart.

I checked the time. 'She should be here' I got up to walk over to Amira's side of the building. I had thirty minutes before I actually started work.

Darcy, my supervisor caught me as I was heading towards the elevator, "We need to chat to put together a game plan for tomorrow" she said as I walked by.

I nodded and smiled as I pressed the button, "Okay, I'll be right back" I said over my shoulder.

I stepped onto the elevator and pressed the nineth floor. Darcy stood there staring at me as I waited for the doors to close, "Come to my office when you get back" she continued to stare me down.

I rolled my eyes as the doors closed. Folks keep thinking their titles give them *the right*. Darcy had proven to be one of those supervisors that's possibly only important at work, hate those type supervisors.

I shook that shit off as I stepped off the elevator. My heels clicked across the floor as I walked to Amira's office. I knocked on her door and she waved me in. She ended her call and jumped up to hug me.

"I've missed you Stink" she hugged me.

Amira had met mu family and was cool, so they allowed her to call me, *Stink*.

"Tyra went on vacation and my sister been in training. I'm so glad you're back" she smiled and did a little dance.

I nodded, "How is Tyra" I smiled thinking about our initial run-in when I used to work on the south campus. Tyra had them girls at that job shook with her sass and spice, you hear me!?! They were scared of Ms. Tyra.

Well, I could get *sassy too,* and I refused to let her get me so when she came to me one day, 'telling me what I needed to do' I stood my *lowest* in seniority' ground and let her know *I wasn't doing it.*

Of course, I paid for it with my supervisor at the time, but Tyra and I had a mutual understanding, I apologized, and she quickly became my girl.

Of course, Amira showed me how I was wrong to have engaged Tyra on the floor in front of folks. But that was so long ago, and like I said Tyra is one my best Boos now. I worked a few shifts with her and realized we were from the same town; she was just a little older. After that, it was all love.

Amira laughed, "We was just talking about you. I was telling her how you told off Lil Bo-Bo the other day" she used a nickname we had given another staff in the building.

I covered my mouth, "Ooo she made me so mad, but this time, I didn't do it on the floor" I said pointing out my growth.

Amira smiled as she thought back to our times on S. Campus. "Girl that's why I am so shocked at you letting Darcy throw her lil weight around on you" Amira shared.

I looked at Amira, "You already know how they play. I'm starting to look like the aggressor but it's me that's going through hell because I wouldn't let Jake talk to me how he talks to the rest of them, but I do my work so what's their problem?" I asked.

Jake is the senior officer in the building. He's managed to work his way through the ranks by being a good ole boy. Jake let it be known upon my first week in the office, he wasn't on board with hiring me. I knew from that conversation I would have it out with Jake, and I did.

Jake thought because I was a young, brown skin girl with an address 'from da Bay' I didn't deserve to be there. I didn't need to get the benefits that were set up to give him a kush life. Well, I nicely let him know, sure did get him straight one day, which backed him up off me. Jake left me alone, until Darcy got promoted to our department. Now they all come at me through her.

Amira nodded her head and flagged me off, "Their issue with you isn't work-related. But enough about them, tell me about ya lil boo thang" she peeked at me from behind her monitor.

I fell back into my chair. "Girl I can't stay long, Darcy wants to 'game plan' site visits tomorrow" I did the air quotes gesture.

Amira put her hand up as her phone started ringing. "I'll be back for lunch" I got up to leave.

"Why is your best friend calling me" she glanced at me and picked up the phone.

"Hey Darcy" Amira made the vomit face as she took the phone away from her ear, "Nope Darcy she left, so she should be down your way" she hung up the phone.

I couldn't believe it. "Are you serious, she called looking for me? I'm early, I don't *log in* until eight, is she forreal?" I waved my hand.

I walked out the office towards the stairs. I quicky stepped down the stairs and walked down the back hallway then came thru the back of the office. I walked across the kitchen and cut down the aisle to my cubicle.

I heard Darcy asking the girl at the desk if I had returned yet when Terrence, my work brother yelled over the cubicle, "Yeah, she's helping me find a judge for my warrant and showing me a file for my new case" he said.

Darcy's voice fake perks up as she walks to my cubicle. I peeked around Terrence standing next to me pretending to read a list.

"Oh MaJhonnie, when you're done come see me" she said very pleasantly and walked into her office.

I rolled my eyes as I slid my cardigan on and walked over to her office. Terrence told me to 'Be easy' and I rolled my eyes hard before I knocked on her office door.

"Have a seat" she pointed towards the chairs by her desk.

"I *thought* I asked you to come see me when you came back" she said firmly.

I looked at Darcy because I wasn't sure if she was trying to check me because she just saw me at my desk 'working with Terrence' but I gave her the benefit of the doubt.

"I was but then Terrence asked me..."

"That's right, he asked for your help" she said cutting me off.

Darcy's tone was sounding a bit facetious, but I blew it off as she began to ask me my protocol for site visits. I explained it perfectly and even offered to help maneuver us at the sites tomorrow, once she expressed, she had concerns.

"Well, you know how custody can be, so do you follow their protocol?" she asked.

I explained to her how I had my own set-up with custody, I even offered my approach.

"I can start my process this afternoon to help us get around faster tomorrow" I offered.

If she agreed, it means she would have to follow my lead, which technically is what is supposed to happen during site visits, she's supposed to be observing me do *my thing* during site inspections, but Darcy also likes to flex on custody staff.

Darcy scoffed at me, "Excuse you, I have been here for over twenty years, I am a Director, I can most certainly get us through these facilities in enough time without any issues, thank you very much" she spat.

I took her snappy response and shrugged it off. Refusing to engage, plus I was already on thin ice after I almost got into it with another co-worker. I decided these people were not worth my energy.

"So, do you want to meet here then ride over together or would you rather meet me at the first site?" she asked.

I quickly agreed to meet her there, "I have to be somewhere right after work on that side of town, so I'll drive my own car" I stood up but paused, "Is there anything else?" I asked sitting back down.

Darcy took in a deep breath, "Just a few more things, try to cut down on your time on the nineth floor, we've been getting complaints" she said tapping her pen against her book.

I looked at Darcy. "Ok" I nodded as I gathered my book, pen and phone to prepare to leave.

I was hot! Everybody in our office be all over this building, why is she so worried about me?

'And complaints? Really?! She ain't getting no damn complaints!'

Darcy directed me she didn't have anything else but wanted me to know, she had started a lunch schedule to keep someone in the office for coverage.

"Your lunch time will depend on the slots that are left. The office picked when you were off last week" she held out a calendar and of course I'm going to be eating at eleven in the morning aka breakfast or two in the afternoon aka last call.

"But I come in at eight, I'm not trying to eat lunch that early. I eat breakfast at home" I objected.

"Do we really need assigned lunch times? I mean some days, I eat lunch at different times, it depends on my workday. Sometimes, I just eat at my desk to get my work done" I started to explain.

Darcy nodded with that fake smile pretending like she's listening and really cared. I listened to her basically flex on me.

Her real issue is since I won't engage with the people in this office, most importantly her and her corny crew like how I've engaged with others in the building; she's going to limit my movements.

I smiled and got up to leave, "See you tomorrow" I said.

"Please tell me you're not going to have those shoes on tomorrow" she made mention of my high heels.

I swallowed down my words and I turned to Darcy, "No, when I do site visits, I wear different shoes" I said looking at my feet.

She had the nerve to stick her foot out showing me her favorite shoe; these kitten heels that she has in every color.

"Do you even own a low heel? I don't think I've ever seen you in a heel that didn't look like you were going out to a club" she said still flexing her foot in that shoe that a grandmother would wear.

"Yeah, I own some very nice Mi-Mi's" I said with a smirk.

"Mi-Mi's??" she asked confused.

"My grandmom, she wears kitten heels; flats and shoes like so" I pointed to her foot. "That's what I call that type of shoe" I explained.

I tucked my lips and raised my shoulders as I spun on my high heels to leave, "See ya tomorrow" I repeated and kicked my foot behind me.

I walked out back to my cubicle. "Fuck her" I said loudly enough as I sat down at my desk.

I checked my phone and barely dodged getting hit by a bite sized Pay Day candy bar that Terrence threw over the divider.

"Chill Cannon" he said.

I picked up my phone, "This day can't move any slower" I smiled at Rafiq sending me pics. "Awww I miss him I need to go visit" I said a loud.

"Ayo, you just got back from a three week leave" he said.

"Don't worry about what the fuck I be doin" I said playfully.

"Yea, a'ight" he laughed.

I put my earbuds in, which helped me focus and I breezed thru my computer work from the last three weeks. I typed up my reports for court dates in October and November. I put my stuff in Annie, the office manager's box for filing.

Before I realized the time, Terrence was shutting down his computer.

'Damn it's four already?!'

I took my earbuds out and packed my bag to go home. "Annie, I'm leaving early tomorrow, I didn't take a lunch" I announced as I turned off my computer and walked out of the office with my work brothers, Terrence and Justin.

I was walking to my car when Lamont, an old fling that won't stay flung; ran over to me.

"Where you been" Lamont asked pulling me into a hug.

He smelled good. Lamont was tall with a slim build. He is your typical office dude. You know he dresses really nice, always going on a boy's trip, never want a girlfriend but want boyfriend treatment because he *has* to keep his options open.

Me and Lamont had been doing *it* off and on for a couple months. He's was cool but Rafiq was better, it was not even worth comparing so I ended it with Lamont.

"No thank you, I got site visits with Darcy tomorrow. I'm going to bed tonight" I said declining his offer to come over,

Lamont joked as he ran off to meet up with another girl. They walked to the train together. I had to shake this feeling off, you know that self-blaming feeling of 'what the fuck was I looking at and going through, when I dealt with him!'

Oh my god, he was so corny to me now.

I pulled out the parking lot, 'Play Raheem Devaughn, I need some lust in my life' I pulled into traffic and zoned out.

I decided it was time, I scrolled through my contacts and called the woman I've called 'Mom' for the last twenty-three years. The phone rang twice and then went to voicemail.

"Oh" I ended the call and pulled into the store parking lot.

I hurried up and grabbed a few items, I was prepared to pay for my groceries, but the cashier told me it had been taken care of, someone had paid for my stuff.

"Aww, I knew I shoulda got them lobster tails" I snapped my finger as I loaded my groceries into my cart.

As I waited, I looked behind me and saw an elderly man in line with a few items.

I scanned his food and handed the cashier fifty dollars. "Here, this is for him *and* you can keep the change, enjoy your day" I smiled as I walked out of the market.

That felt good...

My older brother, Boy was standing by the door as I walked out. "Whaddup doe Lil Sis" Boy said as he spit onto the street. "My peoples looked you out right?" he asked.

I nodded as he put my bags in the car. "Oh, that was you, good look! But I wound up using my money anyway, I paid for the ol man behind me and let her rock out with the change" I said.

Boy closed my trunk "God's gon bless you" he chuckled as I walked around my car.

Boy told me to get home and kissed my cheek, "I'm still trippin' out, I got a not so lil sister" he smiled and backed away from my car. "My first job is to get ya ride cleaned! Why y'all women be so hard on cars?" he asked.

I objected and invited him to dinner on Thursday.

He nodded, "Where you wanna go, I got it" he said.

I shook my head, "No, Ima cook" I said rejecting his offer.

"Oh, hell yeah" Boy swung his arms in front of him.

I honked my horn and headed towards the exit.

I got home and found my care package from Lo had finally arrived. I knew he was gonna get me right. Lo got me some gummies and brownies along with a couple jars.

Logan was turning out to be a bomb little brother. He brings me gift cards from different stores that I like, he always has connections with somebody in the mall. He's been giving me care packages of edibles and other treats. And I can almost guarantee money every time I see him. I go through his pockets, I do a lil shake down on him.

I walked into the kitchen and saw Rebecca standing at the fridge. "I swear I love this juice. Can I have it" she asked taking it out of the refrigerator.

I flagged her, as I kicked my heels off and ran over to rub her belly. I talked into her stomach and she turned her back to me, "No, because why I only get to know you're back because Lo needed me to drop this off" she pointed at the care package.

I hugged Rebecca's back as I apologized for not calling her. I explained how I got home last night, "Girl I would have been in an Uber if I didn't walk out as Pudd was being dropped off, he was going in as I was coming out. Logan brought me home. That's when I put my order in" I finished with a shrug.

Rebecca scoffed and back hand waved at me as she waddled around the counter. "Girl and you're only five months" I smiled as I slid over to my box.

"Girl six, probably because my fat ass still be in there sampling Pudd's non weed infused goodies at two in the morning, just greedy. He is making a killing, if you can't tell from looking at me" Rebecca laughed as she danced around.

"He makes this chocolate like pound cake. Levi said wait until I have the baby, he gon get me one with the chocolate drizzle sauce! It is everything" she hit the counter.

"So, you ready for this" I leaned over the counter.

Rebecca pulled out the stool and climbed up on it.

"You're making me nervous, you got it" I put my arms up, praying that she would not need me to catch her.

Once she was settled, I walked back around the counter, "So one of Rafiq's best friends is a girl that likes girls, well she came at me in the dressing room" I shared covering my face.

Rebecca turned around to face me straight on, "What do you mean, 'Came at you" she asked with her eyebrows raised.

I dropped my head remembering Rebecca loves to hear details about girl-on-girl activity, but she swears she doesn't like girls.

"Yea, you'd love Ness, I'd even introduce y'all if you weren't with my brother and you know the whole baby thing" I said.

"Um excuse me what do you mean if I wasn't dating your brother, how bout I don't like girls" Rebecca objected.

I looked at Rebecca, "Ness would eat you alive, literally" I laughed as Rebecca appeared intrigued.

"So, back to my story; I'm thinking its Rafiq coming in because he keeps telling me he wants to do it in the dressing room" I explained.

"Oh shit" Rebecca starts to bounce in her seat.

I nodded my head, "Girl, I'm leant over like so unbuckling the shoes. You know I hate panties! So, again I'm bent over like so, ooch all out" I waved my hand across my backside as
I demonstrated for Rebecca.

"So, it wasn't the tip of her tongue in my crack, because like I said, ole dude a whole freak and that's his twist" I paused and looked at Rebecca.

I hit the counter, "It was her nails spreading my cheeks that made me stand straight up and turn around. Man, I put that hoe against the wall by her *neck*" I held my forearm in the air.

Rebecca opens my cake dish and picks up a donut. "And then *whattt?*" she asked in awe as she put a piece of the donut in her mouth.

"Girl, I told her if she didn't get the fuck away from me" I hit the counter.

Rebecca gasped, "Oh well now I see why you needed a care package, so how did this end" Rebecca pointed at counter, "Can you give me my juice, so then what you say?" she asked.

I slid the bottle over to her. "I said, 'Don't get me wrong I have thought about riding your face as Rafiq rides my ass but quickly decided if I ever did do that, it would *not be with you*" I repeated my words to Rebecca.

Rebecca gasped in her normal dramatic fashion.

I quickly objected, "What? No, she be turning out bitches in bathroom stalls of dirty bars like naaaw I'm good" I dusted my hands together.

Rebecca leaned back, "You always tryna throw some shit in there real quick, *bitch* circle back to these thoughts of a threesome" she ate more donut.

"I don't think I want a threesome, but I do want that feeling of being sucked and licked while I'm grinding on it" I explained.

Rebecca flagged me. "Ima get you a toy, next time you or Rafiq can work the toy while he's down there working his tongue" she laughed as she clapped her hands.

"Just nasty" I shook my head as I looked at Rebecca.

She shrugged, "My baby be ready" she said popping.

I shuddered at the thought as I ran water into my kettle, "So wait there's more" I announced.

Rebecca sighed, "Oh goodness" she put her head in her hand.

"Well, you already know his godmom is supposedly my mother aaannnd Uncle Junie not really my uncle oh and somehow Fi and Dean *were* together because according to 'yo baby daddy's paperwork Dean is all of our Dads like 99.9999% our dad" I shared.

"Daaammmnnn, well what else can go wrong?" Rebecca asked.

I really wish she didn't ask that question...

… WELL, AIN'T THAT SUM SHIT?!?

SPRING 2021

ABOUT THE AUTHOR

Honestgyrl Lemon aka 'Migs' is a sociologist in education w/specialties in social services and therapeutic rehabilitation. Being equipped with a BA degree in Sociology, and over eighteen years in the correctional/behavioral/mental health field, she's seen and experienced a lot.

Migs, not only creates fiction novels, but she's also created anger and emotion management-based content, healthy relationships/marital guidance, recovery and crisis management. She's also developing an employment readiness and business support coaching program (*ADHDPreneur- one who has a lot of different business ideas but struggles with 'making it all make sense')

'Migs' created the idea of the series, "You Can't Make This Stuff Up" over sixteen years ago. The first book, 'Lies always rise…, was created with the goal to give a vivid picture of how 'emotionally-based' decisions can have lasting affects/effects on the family dynamic.

Born in the Midwest, raised in the Tri-State area of NJ, NY & PA, Lemon has combined her education and life experiences to create a multi-dimensional perception to aid others in their ability to recover while in transition.

She is the Founder of -an HONESTGYRL BOUTIQUE LLC, a place of support for the professional

www.ingramcontent.com/pod-product-compliance
Lightning Source LLC
Chambersburg PA
CBHW050458110426
42742CB00018B/3292